I dedicate this book to my parents.
They are dearly missed, not forgotten, and their legacy of love, honour, and kindness lives on.

Also

In memory of the great Zig Ziglar.
Friend and mentor 1926 – 2012.

Brian Sterling-Vete's
Mental Martial Arts®

Published by

MajorVision International

2024 Edition

Copyright Notice
© 2010 Brian Sterling-Vete All Rights Reserved
Revised, updated, and re-released in 2024.

All material in this book is the property of, copyrighted, and trademarked to Brian Sterling-Vete and Helen Renée Wuorio and/or MajorVision Ltd; unless otherwise stated, A E & O E. Copyright and other intellectual property laws protect these materials. Reproduction, distribution, or transmission of the materials, in whole or in part, in any manner, without the prior written consent of the copyright holder, is prohibited and is a violation of national and international copyright law.

www.BrianSterlingVete.com – www.HelenRenee.com

Contents

Page 09 Chapter 1: Preface and Introduction

Page 22 Chapter 2: How it All Began

Page 25 Chapter 3: Concepts to Consider

Page 67 Chapter 4: The Mental Martial Arts Mind

Page 79 Chapter 5: Communication

Page 127 Chapter 6: Conflict Resolution

Page 163 Chapter 7: Crisis Media Management

Page 191 Chapter 8: Handling Negative Social Media

Page 197 Chapter 9: Confidence, Character Flaws, and 'Stuff'

Page 213 Chapter 10: Leadership

Page 225 Chapter 11: Toolboxes and Tactics

Page 243 Chapter 12: Success - A Journey, NOT A Destination

www.BrianSterlingVete.com – www.HelenRenee.com

Chapter 1: Preface and Introduction

*A Literal Translation of **Mental Martial Arts:***

- 武 **Mental** = Intellect, Combinations of Thought, Perception, Memory, Philosophy, Emotion, Will, Imagination, and Cognitive Processes. The thought processes of reason.

- 武 **Martial** = War.

- 武 **Arts** = The Study of.

Therefore, the definition of my system of Mental Martial Arts is:

The Intellectual and Philosophical Study of the Art of War

All interactions in life, at work, in business, and when negotiating and communicating with others involve an exchange of energy, power, and influence.

In these interactions, both parties try to exert maximum influence over the other party to reach their desired outcome of the engagement. However, one party can always exert greater influence and power over the other. Just as in the physical world, there is always one person who is stronger and more powerful than the other, and the more powerful and persuasive of the two parties will usually be the winner.

A physical analogy would be that of a bigger, stronger, and more powerful person gaining influence over a smaller, weaker person by bullying, intimidating, and even using physical violence. The outcome of such an encounter is usually a foregone conclusion unless the apparently 'weaker' person is trained in the martial arts.

My system of mental martial arts embodies the same strategies and tactics as physical martial arts, providing the practitioner with the verbal and intellectual equivalent of those arts.

The highly effective verbal and intellectual life-combat skills possible with this system can help to redress the balance of power in virtually all interactions. It allows the apparently 'weaker' party to gain an advantage over the much more powerful opposition.

Another valuable ancient Chinese proverb to consider the deeper meaning of this point is: When one tiger avoids another tiger, does this make it the weaker of the two for doing so? Or is it because both are extremely powerful, so there would be no ultimate winner in a conflict? The action of avoiding conflict wherever possible is not cowardice; it is simply the love of life, peace, and harmony.

This leads me directly to one of the most essential points to remember about any aspect of potential combat, either physical, verbal, or intellectual. It is always better to win a war by not fighting a war.

Therefore, an extension of that concept is that it is always better to win a conflict by not conflicting with others. This may sound simple and easy to understand, and I am sure many people will agree wholeheartedly. However, instinctively practising it in all things in life, love, and business usually proves extremely challenging.

Many people allow their egos, emotions, and thoughts of what other people might think about them to rule and control their actions. These are typically the reasons why people from all walks of life, including those who lead nations, are often led down a pathway to destruction and conflict.

One of the greatest gifts you can give yourself is to learn how to instinctively remove your ego and emotions from all interactions and view all the information you receive as mere data. Unfortunately, people always tend to react when, instead, they should learn to respond. In later chapters, I will cover these concepts and why they are crucial to your success.

Chapter 2: How it All Began

For those interested in learning how I first conceived my concept of Mental Martial Arts, I will start at the beginning of my journey in physical martial arts when I was 12 years old. I will also begin by giving you a brief overview of the physical martial arts, how they developed, and how they led me to my concept of MMA. Also, to make it easier, from this point forward, I will always refer to my system of Mental Martial Arts simply as 'Mental Martial Arts,' or MMA. Naturally, this should not be confused with other systems such as Mixed Martial Arts, AKA MMA.

Many different systems of physical martial arts exist today, and I do not doubt that many more hybrid systems will be developed in the future, too. None are better or worse than the other; they are merely different. More importantly, the effectiveness of each art is dictated by the practitioner of the art, not the art itself. In physical martial arts, there is no absolute right or wrong way of doing something; if it works and is efficient, then keep it and use it. If something does not work, then ditch it and forget it.

Like physical martial arts, Mental Martial Arts is not a singular system. They're a collection of various systems, some formalised in this book, others remaining conceptual. The key, as with any physical or mental martial art, is its practicality and effectiveness in real-world scenarios. The focus should always be on what works and what doesn't, discarding the ineffective.

Contrary to popular belief, many of the common Chinese martial arts systems were not originally devised and developed in the Shaolin monasteries. These fighting arts predated the establishment of the monasteries. However, the Shaolin masters played a significant role in incorporating and refining many of these techniques and systems into their own martial arts systems.

The Shaolin masters originated from the Shaolin Monastery or the Buddhist Shaolin Temple, founded in the 5th century AD and located near Zhengzhou City in the Henan province of ancient China.

'Shaolin' literally means 'monastery-temple in the woods of Mount Shaoshi.' Today, there are many Shaolin Masters who visit Western nations to demonstrate their spectacular skills and abilities. However, few teach the art together with the philosophy behind the art.

The peaceful Shaolin monks came together in the monastery, seeking to live in peace and harmony with nature and the world around them. Unfortunately, it was not always possible to maintain peace and harmony in feudal times, which were often war-torn. Therefore, the various systems of Shaolin Kung Fu originated to help maintain peace.

The Shaolin monks studied the combat systems of animals and other creatures, including the snake, praying mantis, monkey, crane, mythical dragon, and, of course, the tiger. They also studied the combat methods, strategies, and tactics of ancient greats, such as Sun Tzu, who is still revered today as one of the greatest military leaders of all time.

Over time, the monks realised that each creature they studied taught them a unique and highly effective method of combat. It is believed that a Shaolin monk once commented that "there were as many different styles of martial arts as there are leaves on the trees."

At first, every method appeared to be quite different from the others. This is good because all people are different, and everyone has different physical strengths, weaknesses, and characteristics. Therefore, people are better suited to some martial arts styles than others, and these factors must be carefully considered. For example, Taekwondo is an excellent Korean martial art. However, it's probably not the ideal choice for a new student in their mid-60s who has lacked lower-limb flexibility. This is because Taekwondo can involve a lot of dynamic high-kicking techniques, including the practice of jump-spinning kicks and flying kicks. However, that person might be better suited to practice the Japanese art of Aikido. This art does not involve dynamic kicking techniques; instead, it concentrates on blending with and redirecting the attacker's energy. Aikido requires the practitioner to have comparatively little lower-limb flexibility compared to Taekwondo.

Some martial arts systems had very colourful and exciting names, such as Drunken Monkey, White Crane, Praying Mantis, Dragon Style, and the famous Tiger Style. The Tiger-style system I originally learned is called Pak Mei, sometimes pronounced Bak May. The name means 'White Eyebrow' and is named after the Shaolin monk who invented the system. There are no prizes for guessing the colour of his eyebrows!

Kung Fu is now used to describe Chinese martial arts collectively. However, the literal translation of the term 'Kung Fu' is derived from the word Kung, or Gong, as it is sometimes referred to, which means 'achievement.' This is combined with the word Fu, which means 'mankind.' Therefore, the literal translation of the term Kung Fu would be: 'achievement by mankind.' Perhaps in Western terms, for those who speak English, it would be best translated to mean: 'human achievement.'

Today, there are as many different martial arts styles as there are teachers. This is because when students become teachers, they always add something new to the art, something unique to them.

When I began my journey in the physical martial arts, it was very much born out of necessity because I grew up in and around the inner-city districts of Rusholme and Moss Side in Manchester, England. At the time, these were some of the toughest parts of Great Britain, perhaps even Europe, and they were rife with gangs of vicious thugs.

My family was small compared to others of the time, consisting only of my parents and me. We may have been monetarily poor, but we were incredibly wealthy in our love, contentment, and happiness as a family. Even though money was usually scarce, my parents always maintained the highest standards of morals, good housekeeping, good manners, and respect for others. Thankfully, these same qualities were passed on to me by my parents, who were my inspiration as a teenager, and they still are to this day.

In the late 1960s and the early 1970s, the area where I grew up as a boy was still being slowly regenerated after the devastation of World War 2. Manchester was hit extremely hard during the wartime blitz because it was one of the leading centres of Britain's industrial heartland, and Hitler wanted to destroy it. He tried extremely hard to do this with relentless blitzkrieg bombing, which happened each night for many years.

My parents instilled in me an element that has been lost by many through the years: wartime spirit. Britain was bombed relentlessly by Hitler's Luftwaffe for many years, and during that time, the people of Britain developed what has become known as the wartime spirit. This is the spirit of cheerfulness under adversity, adaptability, courage, and never surrendering. The whole nation seemed to develop this spirit during World War 2 naturally. Eventually, no matter what hardship and loss they endured, the people still managed to pick themselves up every time they were proverbially knocked down, smile, and keep moving forward. My parents were young people during World War 2, and because they grew up with this spirit, they passed it on to me, and I am eternally grateful for that. Thankfully, Hitler ultimately failed.

Even though I did not realise it at the time, the result of one of Hitler's bombs had done me a huge favour when it destroyed the old factory across the road from my school. The crater left by the huge bomb had created what I considered to be my boating lake, complete with an island made of rubble in the middle.

Despite living every day in the aftermath of debris left from World War 2, we were all incredibly happy with life in general. Furthermore, we even considered ourselves extremely lucky to have two days of summer holiday each year when we would travel away from the city. One of the days was usually spent in the Victorian seaside resort of Southport, best known for being a seaside resort with no sea. This is because of the massing of sand dunes, making the town almost an inland resort. The other day of our summer holiday was almost always spent in Blackpool, famous for its Blackpool Rock. This is not rock in either the geological or musical sense. It is a stick of hard, mint-flavoured candy, which somehow has the word 'Blackpool' written through the core of it!

Heald Place Primary School was an exceptional place for me, and it left a happy mark, indelibly graven on my recollection. I have often heard it said that memories of a great teacher will stay with you throughout your life. Hindsight has proven this true for me because of my primary school teacher, Mr Elmett. He was a wonderfully positive influence on my life, and I think of him often, together with fond memories of life at my old school. Sadly, I have never seen him since that time.

However, Burnage High School vastly differed from the halcyon times spent at primary school. Life there was initially a mixture of pain and pleasure for many reasons, mainly because it was during those early teenage years when the relentless bullying began. As always, bullies are nothing more than mindless thugs and are usually found in gangs to give each other moral support. Unfortunately, the gangs thought that I made a good target for their 'sport.' Why? Simply because I was perceived to be different from most of the others in my peer group.

The first difference was that I did not want to join any of their gangs to bully others, and I did not use foul language either. Instead, I valued studying hard at school and working hard in my first job as a paper delivery boy to earn my pocket money. Another difference was that I was physically very slim in my early teenage years. In fact, when I was 12 years old, I could have been the poster child for the classic '98 lb weakling' as seen in the newspaper adverts for bodybuilding courses at the time!

I am almost certain that this combination of factors led directly to my being bullied. Over time, the bullying increased in both ferocity and frequency and on one occasion, the beating I received by a gang of thugs was so bad that I only narrowly avoided being hospitalised. The gang was led by a particularly large, but in hindsight, cowardly boy. The beating I received from the 5 'brave' boys left me with a black eye, a broken nose, several deep cuts on my head and face, bruises all over my body, and cracked ribs from being kicked while I was on the ground.

Although I certainly did not realise it then, this would be a pivotal moment in my life. That beating was so severe that it meant that I could no longer hide the injuries I had received from my parents. The truth about me being the victim of extreme bullying would now have to be revealed. However, I was still extremely cautious about telling my parents how long it had been happening. If they had learned the truth about that and about how badly I had been beaten at times, they would have gone berserk.

My Father was the real catalyst for changing my life forever in the most positive way imaginable. Realising that bullies only respond to strength, my father decided I should learn to defend myself. Even though he had been an accomplished boxer while serving with the Royal Marines Commandos during the war, he thought I should learn something else. He had spotted a tiny article in a newspaper about a 'new' system of self-defence called Kung Fu. I still possess that same newspaper clipping today, which is very precious to me.

On a Tuesday evening after school, my father took me on one of the old-style red double-decker buses into Manchester centre. I will never forget that journey in late October, just a few weeks before the Guy Fawkes celebrations. As the bus passed along Wilmslow Road, through what is now the world-famous 'Curry Mile,' my mind was racing as I wondered what to expect.

We walked from the bus stop near the Town Hall in Albert Square and onto Deansgate, the premier road in the city. With remarkable clarity, I remember how grand and imposing the ornate Victorian entrance to the Houldsworth Hall appeared to be. However, the interior was a little less impressive because the building was then about 150 years old and looked a little rough in places. The double-door entrance to the main hall was before us, and we paused there instead of immediately entering. My father turned to me and asked me if I wanted to learn Kung Fu for personal reasons and not simply because he thought it would be a good idea, even though this was the pre-Bruce Lee era, and neither of us really knew what to expect. My father also reminded me that once I started something, and if I was committed to it, I should always try to become the best I could possibly be. More importantly, if I committed to learning Kung Fu, I should make it a lifelong journey. I told him that even from the little I had been able to find to read about it, I somehow felt that Kung Fu was meant to be an integral part of my life.

When we walked through the double doors into the main hall, we were immediately greeted by an amazing demonstration of Kung Fu; Sifu George Taylor was about to demonstrate block breaking. Four of Sifu Taylor's students, dressed in black Kung Fu uniforms, held a large piece of old sawn-up wooden railway sleeper. Sifu Taylor stood before the huge block as his students held it with outstretched arms. He paused for a second to take a breath. The next instant, he had punched right through the huge block of wood, just as if it had not even been there. Furthermore, Sifu Taylor punched through the block so expertly that the students holding it hardly felt any impact because they were not shaken in the slightest.

Later that evening, I signed my name on the dotted line to become a Chi Yun Kung Fu Woy member, and I remember thinking about how wonderful it all seemed to be. In hindsight, I had absolutely no idea at the time that I was at the start of an incredible lifelong journey. Not long after I became a Kung Fu student, Bruce Lee would change the world forever, especially the perception of martial arts in popular culture. Thanks to the amazing Bruce Lee and his incredible movies, the Western world would almost 'overnight' develop a seemingly insatiable appetite for all things Kung Fu. I am privileged that I was there at the beginning of it all and lived through the fantastic times as we rode the massive surf of what was commonly called 'Kung Fu mania.' Even today, I clearly remember my very first lesson. I was a young teenage boy who was determined to change his life for the better. I wanted to learn all the skills I needed to stand up to the bullies and stop them from bullying anyone ever again. Even though I was still nursing my physical injuries from the last beating I had taken, it did not matter. If anything, the pain of those injuries only made me train even harder and push myself further. I was a proud student of Pak Mei, or Tiger Tiger-style Kung Fu, and I had a real thirst for learning.

Kung Fu and everything associated with it became my entire life. I was completely motivated, immersed, and enthused by it. Consequently, I trained extremely hard in my martial arts every day without fail. Eventually, I studied several other martial arts, including Karate, Muay Thai, jiu-jitsu, Aikido, western boxing, and even Western wrestling.

I also supplemented my martial arts training with a combination of fitness and bodybuilding exercises with the Hercules 2 mail-order course and later with the fantastic Bullworker to help me develop more strength and stamina. This combination brought about some dramatic results. It transformed me from being the proverbial '98 lb weakling' into an athletic, muscular young man. I became a person that the bullies very soon avoided, and even the gangs of thugs eventually learned to respect me. This was the turning point in my life at school when the bullying and torment by the thugs ceased forever.

Since I was a young man who was still growing, my parents always bought me clothes that were a little on the larger side to make them last a little longer before I grew out of them. So, even though I had been studying Kung Fu for about 18 months and using the Bullworker daily, I did not appear to be any physically different from my classmates due to my loose-fitting clothes.

It was during a lunchtime break at Burnage High School when the showdown finally happened. No matter how hard I tried that day, I could not avoid a confrontation with the biggest bully in the school. This boy was big even by adult standards; however, he did not possess an ounce of maturity or wisdom that his perceived age suggested. He enjoyed projecting his so-called sphere of influence over others, which was generated due to his physical size, and he regularly needed to reinforce that message to help bolster his fragile ego.

During the lunch break, the boy had been writing offensive and obscene words on the chalkboard, probably because he thought it was funny. However, we all knew that our teacher for the next session was a 'no-nonsense' sort, and he would soon be returning to the classroom. Therefore, the bullyboy thought wiping off the offensive words was a good idea. Unfortunately, he also believed that the jacket of my school uniform would be ideally suited for the purpose. I disagreed with him.

In the past, if I had not immediately complied with his request to hand over my jacket, the bullyboy and his accomplices would have forced the jacket from me. They would then have proceeded to do whatever they wanted with it before discarding it like rubbish, leaving me to retrieve and clean it as best I could to hide the damage from my parents.

This time, it was different. When I was told to hand over my jacket, I said "no" in a confident tone, which was something they had never heard from me before. Initially, the bully was surprised and confused at my confident attitude; however, it did not stop him from doing what he would usually do when he did not get his way. He lunged forward at me and took a wide, swinging punch at my head. In the past, the result of such a punch would have probably been that I would be knocked to the ground and would have another blackened eye to return home with.

My instinctive Kung Fu training took over. Even during my comparatively brief 18 months of training, I still had lots of practice in freestyle full-contact combat with some very competent senior opponents. Therefore, I instinctively knew that the bullyboy's attack was strong due to his physical mass; however, I also knew that it was comparatively slow, poorly executed, and easy to deflect.

Using an extremely basic Pak Mei Kung Fu defence move, I engaged his attacking arm while moving forward and sideways, slipping neatly alongside his attack. At that point, my attacker was completely committed to his move. I used his momentum against my opponent as my Kung Fu master had taught me, and helped him extend his lunge forward to send him crashing into the classroom wall.

He hit the wall quite hard with his face and body. This caused him to rebound backwards, falling into the desks and chairs behind him, scattering in all directions as he fell to the ground. He was completely dazed and confused at what had just happened to him. It must have been inconceivable to him that someone he had bullied and pushed around at will for so long had somehow caused this to happen to him with such ease. I could sense that he thought that what had just happened must have been nothing more than sheer luck. So, he stood upright again in such a manner that made it obvious he intended to make me pay dearly for my 'mistake' that had just embarrassed him in front of his friends.

My other classmates who had just witnessed the scene were just as surprised as he was. They stood there in complete silence and disbelief at the events unfolding before their eyes. More importantly, for those classmates who were also former victims of the bullyboy, this was nothing short of pure entertainment. I noticed many of them were smirking and smiling at the treatment the bully was receiving.

Now that the bullyboy was on his feet again, before he launched another attack, he began to hurl obscenities at me as if this would frighten me and cause me to panic. His barrage of colourful expletives told me that he now intended to make me die a horrible and painful death. This was something else that we now completely disagreed on.

In an instant, he rushed forward and attempted to kick me with all his might. Recognising that it was yet another feeble effort to attack me, and since my Kung Fu training also told me that it was a pathetic attempt at a kick, I almost effortlessly engaged his offending leg. I easily deflected his powerful kick by using my leg in a simple deflecting move. This caused him to land rather awkwardly right next to me. Realising he had left himself wide open to an attack, he clumsily attempted to take a backswing at me with his arm. I had already anticipated this move, so I engaged his arm, and once again, I used his momentum to send him crashing to the floor.

I felt mixed emotions about this at the time, but it was beginning to feel like fun. The bullyboy I had feared for so long was now revealed to be someone who was just sad and pathetic. He had shown himself to be more like a three-legged donkey trying desperately to compete in a thoroughbred horse race.

His final attack was equally pathetic and easy to deal with. After once again dragging himself up from the floor, he foolishly tried to kick me again. This time, I engaged and deflected his leg differently, using what is known as a 'limb destruction' technique. Usually, this would involve a blocking move that engaged my opponent's limb by attacking a sensitive nerve point or other vital areas. Instead, I made it even easier on myself and caused his shin to collide full-on with one of the wooden legs of a nearby desk. This left him hopping around on one leg in agony, so I decided to end the incident by delivering a side-thrust kick straight into his stomach. This sent the bullyboy crashing backwards through more desks and chairs to land neatly in the corner of the classroom, where he began to cry profusely as he nursed his shin.

The whole incident must have lasted no longer than 90 seconds, perhaps two minutes at the most. However, as always in combat situations, it seemed to last much longer. That was the end of my being bullied at school forever. More importantly, it was also the end of other innocent classmates being bullied. The bully and his associates never bothered anyone again. They were now obviously too scared even to try.

In hindsight, I hope the bull and his associates learned a valuable life lesson to make them better people in their adult years — important lessons about the fact that people who are forcibly oppressed will eventually fight back. Also, never underestimate your opponent. I believe that the bully's chief life lesson is best summarised in this old Chinese proverb, and I will précis it here: 'Do not despise the snake for not having horns, for who is to say that one day it will not become a dragon.'

From that time onward, for the rest of my schooldays, the most important thing to me was that I was not being bullied anymore. It had also proven that my martial arts training worked exceptionally well in practice. However, later in my teenage years, when I looked back and remembered the scenario from time to time, I began to think about it all somewhat differently. Admittedly, I had won what I liked to call at the time 'the Battle of Burnage High School,' however, I had often wondered if there was a better way I could have dealt with the problem of being bullied. More importantly, I wondered if I could have dealt with it so that I could have avoided physical combat. These were questions that remained unanswered for many years to come.

As the years passed, I progressed ever deeper into my martial arts training. Eventually, it reached a point where it began to shift from being purely physical to including the philosophical aspects of the arts. It was also then that I was first introduced to the concept of it being better to win a war by not fighting a war.

I eventually began thinking that a much more satisfying outcome to 'the Battle of Burnage High School' would have been achieved if I could have defeated the bully without using physical martial arts. I began to think more about physical, emotional, and intellectual energy and how they can all be engaged and redirected using the same principles, tactics, and strategies. However, I also knew that these were skills that I still had to learn.

This could be regarded as the conception point of my system of Mental Martial Arts. Developing this system would involve me gaining much more experience in the physical martial arts and a much deeper understanding of the underlying philosophy underpinning them. It would also require me to undertake a myriad of different jobs and professions as I clawed my way out of being financially poor to become comparatively successful and comfortable in life eventually.

Some of these jobs were safe and fun, such as when I worked selling books in Kendals department store in Manchester. However, other jobs were not always so safe and easy. To earn extra money while studying at university, I worked as a nightclub bouncer in the evenings, patrolling the lonely entrance doors of some of the backstreet nightclubs in Manchester. My great friend Cliff Twemlow would later immortalise the profession of bouncer by referring to it as being a "Tuxedo Warrior" in both a book and a Hollywood 'B' movie. Even though I did not necessarily realise it at the time, I practised Mental Martial Arts almost every night when I worked as a "Tuxedo Warrior," dealing with the ungodly, arrogant creatures of this world. When an incident occurred, I soon learned that it was far better to resolve it without resorting to violence, and it was easier to do this IF I removed my ego from the equation. I also learned that insulting words were mere blows to my ego and would invariably heal much quicker than hard physical blows to my body and face!

Thanks to such experiences, the foundations and principles of my Mental Martial Arts system slowly took shape in my mind. It was like a recipe, with each element of life experience essential to the overall outcome. I progressed enormously in my physical training and competed in many martial arts tournaments. I also competed as a drug-free bodybuilder and even as a powerlifter. During my journey in the martial arts, I am privileged and grateful to have become the recipient of many accolades. I was highly honoured to receive the national Class 'A' Coaching award from the World Karate and Kickboxing Councils and the

International Class 'A' Referee award from the same organisation under Dr Peter Lewis.

Over the years, I have had many jobs and life experiences, all of which helped develop my Mental Martial Arts system. I have experienced military conflict by visiting two theatres of war. During my time with BBC TV News, I was trained by and had bodyguards from the Royal Marines Commandos before being deployed in hazardous places. This was when I also learned many hard lessons and had real-life experiences in the fight against terrorism. I also feel both happy and sad to have experienced the deeply disturbing theatres of civil unrest during the UK race and religion riots of 2001. It was then that I was attacked and set on fire with a Molotov cocktail. Fortunately, my fire protection suit and the Royal Marines who were with me at the time could deal with this without me sustaining serious, lasting injuries. In addition to this, I also found the time to produce 13 World Record events and personally set 5 World Records, which all raised money for charity. My last was a 2005 Guinness World Record, set in Cadiz, Spain, and it raised money for both the Depression Alliance and the victims of the Asian Tsunami.

The result of all of this led to me writing this book about my system of Mental Martial Arts and my coaching people in the system. Eventually, the business world began to sit up and take notice of my new system. They began to understand that Mental Martial Arts could make a significant difference and give them a real edge in commercial terms. It made it possible for a corporate 'David' to defeat a corporate 'Goliath.' In short, it could enable even a small company to triumph over bigger, more powerful corporate opposition.

Typically, my clients are a combination of business executives, education leaders, and politicians. However, occasionally, a celebrity client will need help, too. They all find that one of the most valuable aspects of my MMA is helping them handle the media if they ever encounter hostility, trouble, or scandal. My MMA is ideal in these situations when an innocently used word can be distorted with disastrous consequences to both life and career.

Chapter 3: Concepts to Consider

Dare to be Different.

The concept of 'Dare to be Different' is not just a phrase but a powerful mantra that can transform your life. It's easy to say, yet for most people, it is tough to become genuinely different. Why is this? The answer is that it involves change. Most people are reluctant to embrace change for many reasons, the most common being fear. Fear takes many forms, such as fear of the unknown, fear of ridicule, fear of loss, fear of change, and even fear of success. Fear is often programmed from childhood. This is because, from an early age, a child's mind receives much more negative than positive input. Our parents typically told us what we could not do rather than what we could do. For example, we were often told what we could not eat rather than what we could eat. Even when learning how to cross a road safely, we received negative input by usually being told: "Don't get knocked down." There is also the 'sheep factor' to consider. These people spend their whole lives allowing others to tell them what to do because it is easier that way.

There is also the so-called good advice brigade. These people are only too willing to offer their own seemingly good advice to others. However, their good advice typically projects their negativity and their jealousy. Jealousy may be conscious or subconscious in someone, but it is still jealousy and can have a massive negative impact on others. It is important to remember that most 'supposed' friends do not want you to succeed. That is just a fact. They consciously or subconsciously believe that if they cannot have something better in life, then why should they? We have all heard supposed good advice such as: "You'd better not take chances," and "You'd better play it safe", etc. They are really saying that they do not want you to get ahead in life, and certainly do not want you to get ahead of them. They genuinely do not want you to achieve more than they do, have more than they do, or earn more. They enjoy the status quo of enjoying your friendship without either of you progressing any further. These people like to have you around, typically to call on you when they need to complain about their lack of success.

Even in a relationship with a life partner who is supposed to always want the best for you, jealousy, insecurity, and negative projection can still be present. For example, when one person is insecure, they often project their insecurities onto their partner. In doing so, they tell them what to wear, what to do, how to do things, and, in some extreme instances, what to think.

Therefore, with this massive bombardment of negativity starting at an early age and continuing throughout life, perhaps it is not surprising that most people are genuinely afraid of change.

I like to view the word 'fear' as an acronym: False Evidence Appearing Real. This reminds me that my fears are typically unfounded, and I should have confidence in my abilities and my ultimate success. I believe that one of the greatest crimes to humanity is to see people go through their entire lives with all their ambitions, hopes, and aspirations as nothing more than a dream.

I strongly urge you to ignore the ridiculous confines, pointless restrictions, and negativity that other people impose upon you. Instead, I urge you to always Dare to Dream and Dare to be Different. Make at least some of your dreams become your reality. Your dreams never die on their own; each of us must deliberately kill them for them to die. The choice is always yours.

You are unique, so embrace and savour this fact. You are also not a sheep to blindly follow others. You are endowed with the same capacity for greatness in life, love, and business that everyone else has been endowed with. It is entirely your choice if you use it or not. My Father taught me a fundamental life lesson. This was that if another person can achieve something extraordinary in life, then so could I. YOU can do the same. Have I achieved greatness in life? That all depends upon whom I am compared with. In comparison to some people, I have achieved little.

However, compared to almost everyone, I knew as a child I had travelled more, done more, achieved more, and earned more than nearly everyone I knew. Therefore, it is all relative and measured most accurately against an individual's capacity and resources to achieve rather than against other people's capacity and resources.

The only factor which will guarantee your success is you. You are the best guarantee that you could have. This is because you are always the one who has complete mastery over your future. My point is best summarised by this line from the poem 'Invictus' by the great Victorian poet William Ernest Henley:

"I am the master of my fate; I am the captain of my soul."

No matter what level of success you have already reached, you can always find a new and greater challenge. Commit to memory the well-known phrase: 'Who Dares Wins.' This is the motto of the British SAS or Special Air Service Regiment. The SAS is the original and arguably the finest Special Forces in the world. Also, their motto is very apt because those who dare almost always win in life, love, and business. This approach makes all the difference between winning and losing and between success and failure.

There Is No Such Thing as Failure

Every action will get a result; that is just a fact. The result of that action may not be the originally intended or desired; however, it is still a result. It is just like data obtained from the outcome of a scientific experiment. The processes can be refined in a science experiment to get closer to the desired outcome or achieve it eventually. It would be completely ridiculous to view any results gained along the way as anything more than data that will help you ultimately achieve the desired outcome. Therefore, it is essential to maintain an objective perspective on all aspects of life, love, and business. Taking any other approach is always going to be the pathway to negative self-talk, reproach, disappointment, and perhaps even depression.

In practical terms, to free up your mind from the traditional patterns of fixed thinking that cause you to misread information, it is important to begin by fully understanding that there is no such thing as failure. Failure is merely the result of a course of actions or events, just like in the analogy of science experiments. It is nothing more. It is entirely your own decision about how you choose to perceive and then respond to the outcome, especially if it is undesired.

If you choose to perceive the undesired outcome as something profoundly personal and with huge emotional connotations, then you have a problem. Alternatively, if you choose to perceive the outcome as nothing more than data, you will almost certainly succeed in freeing up your mind from traditional fixed thinking patterns. This is because you have not let your emotions or misperceptions interfere with good judgment.

Therefore, removing your ego from the equation and redefining the traditionally accepted concepts of winning and losing are essential to your success. To quote the great Bruce Lee:

"What is defeat? Nothing but education, nothing but the first step to something better."

Understanding and Controlling the Ego

Since removing your ego from the equation is essential in helping you gain the desired outcome in any engagement, it is worth understanding more about the concept of ego. The word ego is a Latin word for 'I,' or a person's self. Uncontrolled, a disproportionate ego is potentially one of the most self-destructive character flaws a person may possess. It is also a significant mechanism in why a person might become increasingly self-limiting.

People driven by an inflated ego often fall victim to many worthless competitions, and I will explore this concept more thoroughly in the specific section related to winning and losing. For those driven by an inflated ego, there is always a constant battle in their mind to win pseudo-competitions that have no value whatsoever.

This creates a state of almost constant emotional turmoil because it is simply impossible to always be a winner at everything. I know this to be true because I am a Guinness World Record Holder, and as such, there was a time when I was officially proven to be the absolute best in the world at what I once did. However, I also know that someone will always be chasing my crown, and it is up to me if I want to try to win it back continually. If I were to approach life as a never-ending competition, I would only serve to make my life and that of those around me a complete misery.

Those who are ego-driven also need to be perceived as always being correct. This is a particularly destructive quality, and it often fosters associated aggressiveness and unrelenting and annoying persistence. These people would prefer to verbally beat someone into accepting their viewpoint rather than agree to differ. Leaders who possess this character flaw are never in unison with their comrades; they are usually always isolated and alienated.

Ego-driven people also usually have an obsession with constantly seeking the approval of others. One key to success in life, love, and business is the ability to be independent of both the approval and the opinion of other people.

Living in and enjoying the present is an experience that ego-driven people rarely enjoy. Instead, these people often spend their time re-living the former glories of the past and then, at other times, living in the projected days yet to come. They are usually obsessed with what they believe will be the next, better phase of their life. In doing so, they almost always fail to savour the present, which might already be wonderful. It is also rare that an ego-driven person will ever ask for help. After all, they are already the best at everything, right? This is typical because an ego-driven person always wants to take full credit for everything they achieve.

Beware of ego-driven individuals. Also, become aware that certain ego-driven character flaws may hinder your journey to success. To be an effective Mental Martial Artist, it is essential to remove your ego from the equation in all engagements.

Choose How You Perceive Things

The events and circumstances of life, love, and business are never good or bad; they are only ever good or bad because you choose to perceive them that way. This is a simple axiom; however, it is incredibly important, and it can take some people a lifetime to fully understand it. Understanding and practising this concept is vital to your overall success. You must always deliberately, wisely, objectively, and without any external influence decide what is good or bad in your life.

It is also worth remembering that if needed, you can always use certain techniques we will cover later to help you reprogram your perceptions and misperceptions. Since almost everything in life usually has equal advantages and disadvantages, having an objective perspective can help you make better decisions and live a happier life. In the words of the Shaolin masters:

> *"Seek not to know all the answers but to fully understand the questions."*

Logic Will Not Change an Emotion; Only an Action Will

Perhaps you remember how it feels to be a little down or even somewhat depressed? We have all encountered these emotions and feelings at some point in life; it is simply part of being human. I honestly believe that people who say that they have never felt down at any point during their lives either have selective memories or lie about that, and probably other things, too.

The critical question is: How do you change such a powerful emotional expression? You may be surprised that this problem is more straightforward to resolve than you initially imagined. To begin changing your primary emotional state from being sad to feeling happy, you need only perform a simple physical action. The chosen action may not always directly influence what is causing you distress; however, simply performing the action will help start a process of positive change.

For example, the physical action of performing an exercise session will lift your spirits and immediately help you feel less depressed. This is because the endorphins released during physical activity are the body's natural happiness hormones. Therefore, taking positive physical action to get fitter, improve your health, and make yourself look better will help to produce an emotional change from negative to positive.

If you want to change how you feel about something, then take some sort of positive action, and you will immediately begin the change process. Making this simple technique an everyday part of your life will liberate you from unnecessarily experiencing many wasted negative emotions and feelings.

Scientific studies have proven that physical activity effectively changes an emotional state and can even help to beat depression. The case study I will quote was performed by the Department of Psychiatry and Behavioural Sciences at Duke University Medical Centre, Durham, North Carolina, USA.

(http://www.psychosomaticmedicine.org/content/62/5/633.full)

They took 156 volunteers suffering from what was diagnosed as a major depressive disorder, and after a 4-month course of exercise, the results were nothing short of amazing. After completing the short course, patients in all groups exhibited significant improvement, concluding:

"Among individuals with Major Depressive Disorder, exercise therapy is feasible and is associated with significant therapeutic benefit, especially if exercise is continued over time."

There will always be some smart, intelligent people who are depressed, and despite reading the paragraph above, they will still do nothing to change their negative emotional state. They will read the words and understand the science, and some of them may even want to do something, yet typically, they will still do nothing.

What is stopping them? Why do they seem to enjoy a path of self-destruction? There are many reasons why this is. Certain people find their depression a place of comfort, and others enjoy the attention they receive because of their depressed state. Are these people simply lazy? I do not believe that anyone is lazy; I believe that some people merely lack the right motivation. Genuine motivation is critical in changing your life for the better in many ways and achieving greater business success. If you are not completely motivated about whatever you are doing, then change course to focus on something positive that does motivate you.

Make Change Your Friend

Everyone seems to completely forget that everything on our planet is constantly changing, including the weather, the oceans, the ecosystems, and people. This does not even consider any of the social, political, and economic changes constantly happening around us. Even the very planet we stand on is hurtling through space, rotating around the sun in our solar system, which in turn is part of a vast mass of other solar systems which are all rotating around the central point of our galaxy and even our galaxy is moving and rotating with clusters of other galaxies in our universe. Therefore, why are people so surprised that nothing in life is ever fixed, permanent, or solid? Instead, all elements in life are fluid and in a constant state of flux and change.

There are no mistakes in life; instead, only events and opportunities that present themselves. Whether these events and opportunities are a success or a failure does not matter. The fact is that they are all nothing more than data. Therefore, if there are no mistakes, there can be no regrets either. I strongly encourage you to begin to see change as your friend and a new opportunity to achieve more than you already have.

Quote:
"There is only one thing worse than the hardening of the arteries, and that's a hardening of the attitude."

It is important to learn to embrace change since all events in life are merely data. This way, you get to decide for yourself what is either good or bad in life. You will always be the one to decide how you will perceive change, and you will prevent the negative influence of others. However, since our greatest strengths are potentially our greatest weaknesses, it is always wise to be cautious.

An excellent way to approach cautious change is to have what Henry Ford called, 'intelligent ignorance.' He used this phrase when he had his team develop a revolutionary new engine, which was against the advice of the best engineers of the day. The so-called experts of the day told him it could not be done. However, Henry Ford had envisioned a V-8 engine and genuinely believed it could be built. His 'intelligent ignorance' knew that it could be built, and it is for this one reason alone that we now have V8 engines today.

Drawing a Universe Out of Nothing

As a martial arts student, my Shaolin masters taught me an incredible concept: "Never draw a universe from a single word, deed, or action." The deeper meanings behind this philosophy are potent, and over the years, they have positively affected all aspects of my life.

The basis of this concept is linked with the idea of understanding that all the information we receive is nothing more than data. Therefore, it is always your choice how you choose to categorise that data. This, in turn, is also linked to the concept from the book The Four Agreements, which is never to take anything personally. This 1997 influential book was the work of the great Mexican author, Don Miguel Ángel Ruiz. In the book, he urges you to practice the following important concepts daily:

- Be impeccable with Your Word.
- Do not take anything personally.
- Do not make assumptions.
- Always do your best.

Many people waste enormous time, effort, money, and emotional energy by building a complex meaning behind simple data. They let their imagination run wild. To create a complete hypothesis and, in some cases, an entire universe based on nothing other than their imagination. This is a stupid thing to do, yet almost everyone has done it at some time. Furthermore, people often let whatever their current emotional state might dictate what they wish to believe, making it even more bizarre.

Sir Arthur Conan Doyle's great literary detective, Sherlock Holmes, relied upon "Not drawing a universe from a single word, deed or action." His character was often quoted as saying, "Always approach a case with a completely blank mind. Form no theories; simply observe and draw inferences from your observations. It is a capital mistake to theorise before one has data. Insensibly, one begins to twist facts to suit theories instead of theories to suit facts. I never guess. It is a shocking habit, destructive to the logical faculty." I urge you to do the same. This will make your journey in life happier, less stressful, and much more successful.

Win a War by Not Having a War

It is better to win a war by not having a war. This statement is so evident that I should not have to mention it. However, I feel compelled to do so because although this philosophy is revered on the surface, it is quickly forgotten once the menacing cloud of potential conflict descends. Sadly, too many people exercise their ego rather than better judgment, and unnecessary conflict usually results.

By simply removing the element of ego and competition from a situation, you immediately leave yourself open to the possibility of a peaceful solution becoming the natural outcome of a conflict scenario. What is wrong with both sides in an argument, each feeling that they have achieved a victory? As hindsight so often proves, nothing is wrong with that. My Shaolin master taught me this valuable concept when I was a young Kung Fu student.

Over the years and with more profound thought, I eventually felt differently about physical combat being a prime option in a conflict scenario. Ironically, as my skills in the martial arts increased, the less my ego dictated that combat was the only method of conflict resolution available. I eventually reached a point where the thought of physical combat being an option in a conflict became almost abhorrent. It became the very last option I would allow myself to consider. Furthermore, this is probably the same perspective most martial arts practitioners take.

Today, I do not care if the immature and less evolved people I meet insult me or poke fun at me. I do not even think about it because I am secure in my abilities. Therefore, physical combat is hardly ever on my agenda, except when I am training.

I hope that students following my system of mental martial arts will choose the same path because it is the better way. Engaging in competitions that are not real is a complete waste of time, money, energy, and resources.

Competitions such as these are not worth participating in. Remember, a competition is only a competition because we choose to perceive it as such. I will discuss this further in a later section on the concepts of winning and losing.

Do You React, or Do You Respond?

Those who tend to react to situations usually also tend to confuse activity with accomplishment; however, those who tend to respond to situations usually do not. Superficially, the difference between reaction and response may seem small and insignificant. However, it is not. Learning how to recognise if you are reacting or responding to something is a key differentiator between those who succeed or fail in life, love, and business.

I will use an example based on medication to demonstrate my meaning and the differentiator. Imagine that you have a loved one who is ill, and the doctor has prescribed medication. However, after they take the medication, the doctor then tells them that their loved one is reacting to the medication. Naturally, this would be bad news. Alternatively, if, after taking the same medication, the doctor tells you that your loved one was responding to the medication, then that would be an excellent thing. The difference is simple, and it may be small in certain ways. However, there is a huge difference overall.

We all have choices in life, and I strongly urge you to learn how to respond to all things rather than react. How do you break the habit of reacting to things and learn to respond instead? You do this by examining how you approach everything you do. If you are reacting to something out of habit, you can deliberately change it to become a positive response. Once you have started doing this, it takes only 21 days to form a new habit, so it will not take long to change this base mechanism forever. Once you have made it your habit to respond, the associated thought process will soon shift from your conscious mind to your subconscious. This is like installing a software patch in a computer's operating system.

Activity vs. Accomplishment

Using a physical action to modify feelings or emotions is a valid technique. However, there is a potential danger that you should always be aware of. This is to confuse activity with accomplishment. This is an easy mistake to make and a common one, too.

We have all seen people who allow themselves to react rather than respond to a situation and let their emotions overrule their good judgment. These people usually waste precious time, energy, effort, and money just because it feels better to do something rather than nothing. In a stressful scenario, doing something simply for the sake of doing it is beneficial because it helps relieve some stress.

It is all part of nature's base mechanism to help us cope better in a crisis. However, just because you are doing a lot does not necessarily mean you are achieving a lot. I learned this important lesson early in life as a young martial artist. During mock combat situations, my inexperience often caused me to be drawn into unnecessarily expending my energy and strength. I probably did so simply because there were times when it seemed better to do something rather than nothing. I will never forget those physically painful martial arts lessons, which taught me to recognise the often subtle differences between confusing activity and accomplishment.

The following questions will help prevent you from automatically confusing activity with accomplishment. Before you do anything, try pausing for a moment while you consciously ask yourself the following questions:

- 武 "Is what I am about to do essential?"
- 武 "Will what I am about to do take me closer to my target, or will it take me further away from it?"
- 武 "Is what I am about to do cost-effective?"
- 武 If you are spending on a corporate account, then ask: "Does the money I am about to spend represent good value for the company I work for?"

- 武 If you are about to spend money from your bank account or the joint bank account shared with your partner, then repeat the question above.
- 武 "Is what I am about to do completely ethical and legal?"
- 武 "In the future, will I be proud of what I am about to do?"
- 武 "Will what I am about to do benefit my business, my company, or my family? Or will it merely serve to make me feel better for the moment?"

These questions are an excellent place to start, as they help prevent you from regularly confusing activities with accomplishments. If you answered 'yes' to any of the above, you almost undoubtedly confuse activity with accomplishment. I strongly urge you to take positive action now and stop wasting precious time and money. More importantly, stop wasting other people's time, effort, and money.

Harmony and Balance

Harmony and balance are part of the yin and yang, the balance in the circle and sphere of life. This is where nothing is ever stronger or weaker; it is simply different. They are two essential elements to success in all aspects of life: love and business. However, several aspects of harmony and balance need to be worked on to maintain a true perspective.

No matter how well-balanced you are, you will always encounter destabilising forces when you undertake a new phase of personal or business growth. A good leader is always aware that the first casualty of any campaign is usually the plan. Therefore, you should always expect change to affect your harmony and balance constantly. You should always expect plans to change, people to change, and timescales to change. More importantly, you should also expect people to change their minds about things beyond your control.

The most important difference between success and failure is how well you can handle the forces that affect harmony and balance in all aspects of your life. Everyone needs to learn how to improvise, adapt, and overcome the external forces encountered in life, love, and business.

I began thinking more deeply about the concepts related to adaptation, constant change, and the Yin-Yang factor in a new way when a friend asked me to help move some furniture. My friend had a waterbed and thought he would save time if he only partially drained it. Therefore, its previously fixed shape would swiftly change to adapt to its new surroundings whenever we moved it. The faster the movement, the quicker the shape changes become.

This made me similarly think about life. I began to see it as a river that is always fluid and flexible. It flows from birth to death and constantly changes as the journey progresses. Sometimes, change takes place relatively slowly, so we begin to believe that we have fixed elements in life. However, it is just an illusion because the river of life is still flowing. Change is as much a part of life as the air we breathe, and once you understand this fact, life takes on a new perspective.

More importantly, a simple shift in perspective can dramatically alter your life for the better. It can immediately reduce your stress levels, and you will begin to gain the emotional balance you need to become a better Mental Martial Artist.

This, therefore, begs the question, "How can one find balance and harmony in a constantly changing life and universe?" It is a valid question and one with a surprisingly simple answer. Learn to make change your friend and always respond to change rather than react. No one can fight the flow of change because no one can metaphorically swim against an impossible current. You may be able to resist change for a short while, but not for long. In a river, even the biggest and strongest rocks are eventually worn away and moved by the water flow. Therefore, I believe it is best to learn how to swim or ride the metaphoric surf of the flow of change. In doing so, you should then learn how to channel and direct the energy flow of change. This is the secret to success in understanding and using Mental Martial Arts. To quote an amazing martial artist and close friend, the great John Carrigan:

"Adapt like a shadow. Respond like an echo. Reflect like a mirror. Flow like water and strike like lightning."

In other words, by seamlessly adapting to change, you can instantly respond to opportunities.

Foundations of Balance

Foundations are essential to everything. Everyone needs a solid foundation of personal, social, and business balance. Personal and social balance comes through community activities, time spent with friends and family, participating in sports, and developing hobbies. We all have a spiritual balance, a stance on which we base our beliefs. More importantly, contrary to popular belief, this is not always fixed. Many people's spiritual balance will have grown, changed, and developed throughout their lives.

Professional balance is often the one that causes the most issues. This is because, for most people, this is where it all becomes completely distorted. We spend most of our time each week in a working environment. Since this is the case, if the perspective of your working life is distorted and out of balance, it can seriously affect every other part of your life. Most people know when there is an imbalance in their lives. However, very few do anything to correct the problem before the negative repercussions begin. For many, it becomes all about work and business to the detriment of every other aspect of life. For these people, money always comes before everything else, including their family. Sadly, they typically learn their mistakes the hard way in retrospect.

What does all of this have to do with Mental Martial Arts? Developing a well-balanced social, personal, and business life is like a physical martial artist learning how to create a basic, well-balanced stance. Without a basic, well-balanced stance, martial artists will always underperform. They will always be weak, ineffectual, and generally get things wrong.

An excellent question everyone should ask themselves regularly is, "How well-balanced am I?" For example, how often have you found yourself distracted while at work? Even though you are supposed to be working, you are thinking about and feeling that you should spend more time socially and having fun. Similarly, when you are out socially and having fun, have you ever been consumed by thoughts that you should be working more on your business or career? Again, while finding yourself in either of the two previous examples, have you also ever felt guilty for not spending more time with your loved ones and family?

We have probably all experienced such feelings, and they originate from a lack of balance and harmony at the core of our lives. When our minds wander in this way, the result is that we are never entirely focused on achieving the success we are seeking in life. We are never operating at 100% of our capacity. This lack of focus creates an almost constant emotional confusion about what we are doing at any given time, and we will never be truly living in the moment, either!

The incredibly wise Dalai Lama once taught that humanity sacrifices health to make money. It then sacrifices the money made to recuperate health. Therefore, mankind is usually so anxious about the future that it cannot enjoy the present. Mankind's actions are such that it typically neither lives in the present nor the future. This is instead always living in the moment as if death will never happen. Then, when death finally calls, mankind dies without ever having truly lived.

If your life is out of balance in any way, you need to work to correct that problem before you do anything else. The simple fact is that you cannot move ahead effectively until you have done that. Being in a constant state of emotional conflict is not conducive to success in anything. This state of off-centred turmoil will eventually destroy you through stress, just like an off-centred wheel would destroy a moving car. Unless you find your proper balance, you will always underperform in anything you do.

How to Develop Better Life-Balance

A good starting point would be to develop better objectivity because almost everyone has difficulty being objective about themselves. This will probably always be a 'work-in-progress' throughout your life, so do not expect it to be a quick fix.

Learn not to take things personally and to receive information as data. This action alone will immediately remove many pseudo-issues and problems from your life in general. Learn to minimise the effect of, and if possible, entirely remove, your ego and emotions from affecting all aspects of your life. This is especially important in your interpersonal relationships. This will help enormously because most people are ego-driven, so it can quickly ruin their relationship with their life partner.

More importantly, do not ever accuse your life partner of your imagination. Unfortunately, it is a common thing that people do, and it can ruin a relationship faster than anything. In such circumstances, it is sadly commonplace for people who are inexperienced, insecure, egotistic, and emotionally driven to allow those emotions to overrule good judgment. What people usually accuse other people of, especially in a personal relationship, is typically a projection of something within themselves and has nothing to do with the real issue.

Next, you must re-evaluate the often misguided concepts of winning and losing. Why is it important to always feel like you have somehow won an argument? In martial arts, we learn that sometimes we must give way before advancing. The same is true in life, love, and business. It is also a basic military strategy. Will the world end if you feel like you have lost an argument? No, of course, it will not. However, if you constantly feel strongly as though you have lost an argument, then it is a sure sign that you have some fundamental issues you need to address. These will usually be self-esteem and ego-related issues; some people may even need professional help. In a later chapter, I will cover the concepts of winning and losing in greater detail.

Flexibility and Responsiveness

Perception is the most flexible of all characteristics because your perception will always change to suit your life and your current environment. Perceptions can change quickly, resulting in rapid changes in attitudes, beliefs, and objectives. These can then dramatically affect all other aspects of your life. If your perceptions or misperceptions lead you to form a rigid and inflexible attitude, then you have a serious problem. Emotional flexibility is an essential quality to develop, and it will help you to smooth out some of life's bumps. It will also help you to become a better Mental Martial Artist.

A physical metaphor would be a physical martial artist in combat. They will usually respond quickly enough to deal with an attack situation if they are flexible. If a change of direction is required and a specific movement must be made, the martial artist must do this as quickly as possible. They must be flexible enough to easily and quickly perform the most athletic of moves. The combination of these elements will then usually lead them to win the engagement successfully. More importantly, flexibility will have been a critical element in the equation.

As a practitioner of Mental Martial Arts, you must also be able to do the same intellectually. The quicker you recover from any destabilisation, the greater your chances are of gaining a satisfactory outcome of the engagement. One of the critical factors in determining your overall success will be how fast you and your business can regain your balance after a destabilising event. The destabilising event could have affected you on many levels, including personal, family, financial, social, and business. A serious event may even affect more than one of those elements, perhaps even simultaneously. Emotional flexibility is an important element in effectively dealing with such destabilising events. This is only achieved through positive responsiveness to change and the removal of ego and emotions from the equation.

In today's aggressive business environment, it is increasingly becoming all about the survival of the fittest. Conventional marketing and promotional methods often do not deliver that vital, decisive 'punch.' Mental Martial Arts strategies, tactics, and techniques can help change that. Furthermore, it can help you deliver the essential knock-out 'punch' when needed. Like in the physical martial arts, modern business success is all about sizing up the opposition, engaging them where necessary, avoiding attacks, defending your core business from aggressive new competitors, and seeking increased market share in highly competitive markets.

From a business perspective, some companies are better suited to recovering rapidly from destabilising events. A smaller company that is well structured, flexible, and has good leadership will almost always recover very quickly. Their corporate structure would hopefully reward fluid, adaptive, and creative behaviours. Furthermore, they would almost certainly applaud those who take the initiative rather than those who do nothing except cover their backs. Likely, such a company would not simply recover quickly from a destabilising crisis; it may even make progress by capitalising on new opportunities.

Therefore, it could be argued that the inherent structure of a small—to medium-sized business under good leadership usually fosters all the qualities needed for success. While this is partially true, it is certainly not always the case. Without proper leadership, any business, no matter what the size, might be nothing more than a proverbial paper tiger.

Conversely, the typical structure of a large company is not usually able to respond as fast as a small business would be able to. Large corporate structures are typically cumbersome, slow, and even arrogantly ignorant of their inherent weakness. Most large corporations are about as quick to respond to a crisis and change as the Titanic was when attempting to avoid the iceberg. The leadership of a large company may earnestly desire to move the organisation quickly; however, the inherent corporate inertia usually stops this from happening by default. To make a rapid change, a large company must involve the entire workforce as a team and unite them in a single-minded determination to succeed. Unfortunately, large organisations are typically infected by some individuals who prefer to avoid change at all costs. For many such people, it is almost as if they have retired while at work and remain on the payroll as they coast along.

Another essential factor to be considered is the 'cover their back brigade.' These are the people who usually work invisibly in many large companies. They also achieve nothing more than finding new ways to avoid change and to 'cover their own back' if it is forced upon them. How ludicrous is that? Unfortunately, these people are commonplace in large organisations. They almost learned how to 'cover their back' as part of their MBA course. Is this how empires are built? Is this the way discoveries are made that will change the world for the better? When was a statue last erected of a person recognised for being good at covering their back to save their country? Are these unwritten yet almost revered corporate qualities the stuff of true leadership? It is, sadly, a corporate reality.

I strongly urge anyone who works in a large company or a government organisation to always have the courage to show authentic leadership. To help make changes for the better and to help streamline the business and make it more efficient. Work at eliminating the typically useless layers of worthless protocols and people, like corporate arteriosclerosis. They help to cause inflexibility in the metaphoric arteries of an organisation, which will eventually kill it. If an organisation suffers from any form of corporate arteriosclerosis, then my advice would be to start looking for another job ASAP.

If you are already a leader in such an organisation, then closely examine the structure under you. Do not just settle for the glossy overview presented by corporate 'yes' people on your team. Instead, look more forensically at what is going on. There may be many working under your leadership who are extremely creative and can make a real difference to your business. However, they may be being repressed and in fear of reprisals from those who are slightly senior to them and less capable. To quote my good friend and mentor, the amazing Zig Ziglar:

"Be firm on principle but flexible on the method."

Although failure is never the objective, it is also a part of life, love, and business, so get used to it. Companies that punish failure are the very companies that are ultimately doomed to fail. In punishing the failure of genuine effort and the best intentions of their employees, they are ultimately killing creativity and loyalty. Executives who punish failure are as much of a use as parachutes on submarines. The leadership is the real problem, not the people they supposedly lead.

The final factor that affects balance, harmony, and flexibility is almost always deliberately ignored: political correctness. Political correctness rarely solves a problem; instead, it typically makes everything worse. It may not be immediately apparent, but over time, it is like an abscess that festers to become a bigger problem at a later time.

Furthermore, it disrupts the balance of individuals, companies, and even nations. Therefore, why does corporate and institutional leadership still embrace and celebrate it so much? The reason is that weak leadership lacks the courage of common-sense convictions; therefore, they embrace political correctness initiatives like they would have applauded and embraced the 'Emperor's new clothes' in the fable.

When the system leadership allows the personal beliefs or needs of a group, often in the minority, to completely override the beliefs and needs of others in the majority, the result is always deep-rooted unrest and resentment; it may not always be noticeable, but one can be certain it exists. Whatever happened to the concept of democracy?

Another significant problem is so-called positive discrimination. Typically, this is dressed up with an acronym such as EDI (Equality, Diversity and Inclusion) in the UK, and DEI (Diversity, Equity, and Inclusion) in the USA. The biggest problem with all of this is that no matter how it is dressed up, it is always going to be blatant discrimination and bias based on race and skin colour, all of which is disgusting.

The only real test of any policy like this is if the so-called positive discrimination and bias is only directed against one race and skin colour. If it is, then no matter how it is dressed up, it is a disgusting form of overt racism that has somehow been allowed to become acceptable as something supposedly good. Crucially, anyone who hires someone while following and complying with a DEI/EDI initiative becomes a racist.

Furthermore, any form of DEI/EDI almost always means that the person given the job is never the best and most highly qualified for the job. If you do not think this is important, answer my next question honestly. "If you were forced to undergo critical life-saving surgery, would you insist that the person performing it was hired as part of a DEI/EDI initiative, or would you prefer the best and most highly qualified person regardless of their race/skin colour?" I believe anyone reading this now who answers "Yes" to preferring a DEI/EDI hire is lying. Remember that the DEI acronym might mean Diversity, Equity, and Inclusion to some; however, the DEI acronym can also mean 'Didn't Earn It' because it's probably more applicable, and they rarely have.

Similarly, imagine a military Special Forces unit assembled through DEI/EDI initiatives. They would seldom succeed in achieving any objectives, and if they engaged a meritocracy-based enemy, the DEI/EDI team would need a good supply of body bags. The same is metaphorically true in business.

Lastly, everyone hired as part of DEI/EDI initiatives will always be aware that they almost certainly didn't get the job based purely on merit and their ability, which is deeply psychologically damaging, to say the least. To put it bluntly, DEI/EDI discrimination is like a cancer that will ultimately kill businesses and societies. Maintaining a genuine meritocracy is the only proper, common-sense way forward. Also, showing genuine, unbiased respect to all people as equal human beings would eliminate the belief that enforced political correctness and DEI/EDI initiatives were needed. The Shaolin Masters teach:

"Even the strongest tree can be blown down if the wind is strong enough, simply because the tree is too inflexible. However, the humble blade of grass will always remain to stand because it is flexible to the core."

Preparation Meets Opportunity

If you are fully prepared for any, eventually, when a suitable opportunity arises, success will be the result. It is that simple. Preparation and training in advance are essential elements to almost every aspect of success in life, love, or business.

If your business is prepared, then when incredible opportunities arise, you can take full advantage of them. I am always shocked by the number of people who seem to think that they will only start to prepare and put the infrastructure in place when an opportunity arises. This is much too late and is nothing short of ridiculous, naive thinking. Furthermore, the level of infrastructure typically needed to take full advantage of exciting opportunities usually takes many months or even several years to set into place. Therefore, long-term planning and preparation are essential at all levels.

Belief

A belief is a concept you assume to be true, although you do not know it to be a fact. It is only through the evidence of experimentation and your experiences that your beliefs become your perceived facts. Therefore, if we decide to believe that something is positive, we will also express positive energy and tend to receive positive energy back in return. Likewise, if we decide something is negative, we will tend to express negative energy and receive negative energy back in return. It is that simple: what you give, you get.

An excellent example would be examining your perceptions about parking your car. If you believe you always have trouble parking your vehicle, that is precisely what will happen every time you pull into a parking lot. Furthermore, whenever you think about parking your car, your brain will automatically express the negative energy patterns associated with your negative feelings about those situations. In turn, this will cause stress, and you may even become physically irritated when parking your car.

In short, you will reduce your overall level of performance. Reversing this concept, if you believe that you are always lucky in finding a parking space for your car, and you always have a good experience. The reverse becomes true. Simply because you believe yourself to be lucky, you will always feel good about those situations and happy instead of stressed. Therefore, many people think they have what is commonly referred to as good parking karma, which is nothing more than positive energy attraction.

The same is true about everything else in life, including when thinking about your lifemate. If you feel increasingly negatively about that person, you will subconsciously express more negative energy towards them. In turn, this will subconsciously filter through into other aspects of your relationship until, eventually, every time you think about that person, you have a bad feeling. At that point, you only associate that person with their negative qualities instead of the positive qualities which first attracted you to them. The moral here is to always look for the good and constantly remind yourself of the positive attributes that a person possesses rather than their deficiencies. In doing so, you will generate and maintain positive energy towards them, which will help you maintain a better, happier, and healthier relationship. The great martial arts master Steve Powell once said about the quest for perfection:

> *"I searched the world looking for the perfect woman; however, when I found her, I discovered that she was searching for the perfect man."*

Perception, Belief, and Reality

Since perception is always your reality, it is even more important to always view all your sensory input as nothing more than data, never make assumptions, and not take anything personally. To better understand perception and how it affects your life, I would first like to define and establish precisely what perception is.

In layman's terms, perception is the information your brain receives through physical processes such as sight, sound, touch, etc. Therefore, it is the primary input via one or more of the body's sensory receptors. When you encounter unfamiliar sensory input, your brain begins to process that input based on stored information from past experiences. When enough information has been gathered, your brain begins categorising the data according to familiar data points.

At this processing stage, it becomes common for the stored data points, together with the categorisation of the new data, to become distorted and miscategorised. This is how we create our perceptions and misperceptions. Negative data points are usually created by habitually negative self-talk and other related factors. Over time, and without correction, these perception problems can compound, resulting in character flaws such as extreme prejudices, etc.

An excellent example of misperception becoming a person's reality occurred many years ago when I worked for a while as a stuntman in TV and films. I was working on a TV show in England, and for logistical reasons, there was a car drive between the make-up truck and the film location. One day, after being processed by makeup, I travelled by car with a friend working on the show. At this point, we were both in full costume and makeup. My friend Paul is a big, imposing guy by any standards, and he is a former military man who is as tough as he looks. However, Paul is an extremely lovely, decent, and gallant gentleman, one of the nicest people you could ever meet. On our way to the film location, we passed through a neighbourhood considered a little rough. It was in that neighbourhood, and while we were stopped at traffic lights, we noticed a senior citizen in what appeared to be a broken-down car.

Since we had a little time to spare, we stopped to offer the lady our assistance. We also wanted to reassure her of protection through our presence until we could summon the appropriate mechanical aid. Paul exited our vehicle first and promptly made his way over to the lady. Then, I noticed the expression on the lady's face change dramatically.

As he approached her, she appeared to grow increasingly nervous and agitated. She suddenly scrambled to get back into her car and locked the door. While all this was happening, I could hear Paul politely, in his perfect English voice, "Madam, may I be of any assistance to you?" However, it had become clear that she was not hearing what Paul was saying. Instead, she appeared frightened and gestured to him that he should leave.

Thankfully, the eventual outcome was positive. We called the police for her protection and the Royal Automobile Club roadside assistance, who would attend to her car. While waiting for the emergency services to arrive, it was not long before the nice lady laughed as we all chatted. She had also learned that we were working on a TV show she was a fan of, so she wanted to hear about what it was like to be part of that. Consequently, she also knew why we were deliberately dressed to appear as the thugs she had initially mistaken us for.

This begs the question: Why did she first fear our presence and scramble to get back into her car to lock the door? The answer is simple. The lady's perception was her reality. She saw us, and her perception of our visual image was that of two large and menacing guys.

Her visual sensory data miscategorised the information it received based on previously stored information. Her self-talk had also probably further influenced this process over many years. Therefore, according to her perception, we were simply two thugs, so she decided that her best course of action was to lock herself inside her car. This was a perfect example of how a person's perception is also their reality. Quote:

"Most smart people learn from their mistakes; however, the smartest people learn from other people's mistakes."

Questioning Habits and Beliefs

Most of our beliefs, especially those founded early in life, are passed on from parents, friends, and teachers at school, etc. These beliefs usually remain with us into later life, and we never question them. This is also why most people do things out of habit.

An excellent example of why most people do things out of habit and without questioning the belief behind it was demonstrated to me by a member of staff in my TV production business. At the time, the person had worked for my company for almost fifteen years. One day, while passing through the equipment storage area, I noticed him packing two modern digital TV cameras, which had to be transported via dirt-track roads in Africa, where we were to shoot a documentary.

For some reason, I had never noticed precisely how he had packed TV cameras, especially since he had packed them many times. However, this time, I did notice and was amazed by what I saw. I observed him silently and watched him completely strip down the camera into all the respective parts, including the lens, viewfinder, battery attachments, etc. I was amazed to see him do this because we always carry our TV equipment in Pelican protective cases, which are waterproof and virtually indestructible.

I then asked him why he was stripping the cameras down into their separate parts for shipping, because it was not necessary. At that point, he stopped what he was doing and paused to consider his answer. This was the first time that he had ever given the process a conscious second thought. When he finally did answer, I was stunned by his reply. He explained that he had only realised when I mentioned that the cameras did not need to be stripped down because we now used the Pelican protection cases. He also told me how he had first developed the habit and the associated belief system, which had remained unquestioned for over fifteen years until that time.

Since he had been with my company from the beginning, he reminded me of the early days and the first TV equipment we bought. At that time, we could afford the best camera and sound equipment, but could not afford excellent carrying and protection cases. The alternative was to purchase lower-quality camera equipment to afford better carry cases. However, this was not an option for us, so the choice was simple. Since we always believed in offering the absolute best service and camera equipment, buying the best protection carry cases would have to come later.

Naturally, as we became increasingly successful, we eventually fitted all our equipment with the best protective cases available. However, when we struggled to make the business profitable in the early years, we used anything we could to carry the equipment in. We often used old suitcases with various-sized pieces of foam padding to form an impact barrier. We once even used a padded bag with old towels. Therefore, when we needed to pack the equipment, especially for a hazardous journey, we would always dismantle it into separate parts to protect each piece from potential impact damage during transit.

Therefore, from that time forward, the habit became an unquestioned belief that remained with him for many years.

We should all ask ourselves, "What do I do from habit or belief, which may once have had merit and yet has absolutely no relevance to you today?" Your answers may surprise you as much as my answers surprised me when I objectively asked myself that question.

The Road Trips

I love road trips, and in May of 2011, I embarked on a 3000+ mile road trip with a friend from Poland who was visiting the USA. This trip was planned carefully, and it would take us through some of the most beautiful parts of the country and across several states.

We met in San Francisco, and from there, we drove east to Sacramento, Lake Tahoe, and then down the California-Nevada border, turning through Death Valley to Las Vegas. We then ventured into Arizona and New Mexico before eventually heading over to Southern California and finally driving up the Pacific Coast Highway back to our starting point in San Francisco.

During the journey, we often explored many old trails and small towns off the beaten path. We stopped at one to refuel at a crossroads gas station that was particularly remote, even by our standards, and we were getting hungry. So, I struck up a conversation with the gas station kiosk attendant, who was a girl in her mid-twenties and asked her what bars and restaurants she would recommend either nearby or further along the road. Her reply took me completely by surprise. She told me that she knew little about the surrounding area and certainly nothing about what lay beyond the border of the township where she lived.

She explained that her family house was on the outer edge of the township area, some 15 miles from where she worked, but she had never travelled much beyond that point. I eventually discovered that in her entire life, she had only ever travelled within an estimated 25-mile radius of the township where she lived. She further explained that her parents had once had a bad experience when they first travelled as a young couple, which discouraged them from travelling again.

Consequently, not travelling became their habit, and it was eventually passed on to their children. I then asked her if she had ever considered travelling, perhaps to see something of the wider world outside the township area, especially abroad. Once again, her reply shocked me. She told me that she had little interest in travel and even told me with great conviction that, in general, travel was not safe, so it was best avoided if possible. She had been conditioned not to travel because of someone else's past negative experience. Another person's belief had become her own belief and habit.

Flea Training

The self-limiting beliefs demonstrated by the girl in the gas station reminded me of flea training. To be more precise, the method of flea training an old colleague and good friend, the great British entertainer Michael Bentine, taught me. For many years, Michael was one of the premier entertainers on British TV. On occasion, for a children's show, Michael used a mock flea circus as part of his performance, which intrigued me, so I asked him about this when I met him by chance while I was working at the BBC in London. He explained that he did not use a real flea circus on TV; however, he had learned several interesting facts about fleas during his research for the show.

He then shared a fascinating story about a real flea trainer he had once worked with. The real flea trainer used to train his fleas by capturing as many as possible in a glass jar. Since a flea can jump many times its height, something between 7 and 13 inches, this is the equivalent of a human jumping several hundred feet in the air. Therefore, theoretically, the flea could easily jump straight out of the jar. However, the lid of the jar was not just needed to stop the fleas from escaping; it was an essential part of the training process.

Naturally, the flea has no concept of how high it can jump, nor does it have any idea of being in a jar with a closed lid. Therefore, when they are first put into the jar, the fleas would jump, attempting to escape the confines of the unknown container. Since the lid was in place, the flea would hit the lid and drop back down to start the process again. Michael told me that it did not take long for the fleas' tapping sound when they hit the top of the jar to stop eventually. The flea trainer could then remove the lid from the jar, and even though freedom was now clearly in sight, the fleas could no longer jump out of the jar. They continued to jump, but only to a height no greater than where the barrier of the lid had once been. From that point onwards, no matter how hard they tried, they could not jump any higher than the former barrier.

They had been conditioned to believe they could only jump to a certain height and no further. Many people are similarly conditioned to be restricted by self-limiting beliefs. Our often distorted perceptions usually impose these beliefs, combined with negative self-talk. Alternatively, they are beliefs instilled into us by other people. No matter how the beliefs are created, the effect is always the same. People are often conditioned to reach only a certain limit in life, love, and business and no further. I shudder to think how many people in the world have been conditioned never to even get close to reaching their full potential. I also wonder how advanced humans might be without this restrictive conditioning.

Caterpillars in Cadiz

Concerning examining self-limiting beliefs, I will describe something that happened to me in January of 2005 when I took my production team to Cadiz, Spain. This was where I committed to performing another Guinness World Record attempt, which would be part of the launch of the new medication, Cymbalta, for Eli Lilly Pharmaceuticals. In addition to attempting to set a new Guinness World Record, I delivered a series of seminars on Mental Martial Arts.

In contrast, the rest of my team delivered a variety of team-building exercises. Despite it being January, the weather in Cadiz was balmy and congenial, quite different from what we had left behind in England. Since the weather was so agreeable, we often rehearsed in the open-air sections of our hotel courtyard.

One day, while rehearsing, I noticed some caterpillars on the pavement nearby, so I stopped to watch them. These were not ordinary caterpillars; I recognised them immediately as being Pine Processionary Caterpillars. These little chaps were out particularly early that year because they usually nest high in the pine trees until spring. I pointed them out to my team, and they all stopped rehearsals to watch the line I was referring to. I then explained a curious fact I had learned about these caterpillars. As their name might suggest, once set into motion, the Processionary Caterpillar will always follow the one in front, forming a line or procession. If you were to guide the leading caterpillar, turning the line into a circle so that it then faced the rear of the last caterpillar in the line, the procession of caterpillars would then walk around in a circle.

I did exactly that and set the line of caterpillars walking around in a circle on the pavement. Curiously, they would never break the circle of their own volition, and they would literally starve to death hunting for food in this way. I knew that their favourite food was pine needles, so I placed a small portion in the centre of the circle of caterpillars.

Their favourite food was now only inches away, and they could certainly smell it, yet they never once broke ranks to leave the circle and find the food. I eventually set them free and led them to their favourite meal, so all was left as it should be. I now have some questions for you:

- 武 "How have you been conditioned to only reach a certain limit in life, love, and business?"
- 武 "What are you going to do about it, and when?"
- 武 "What do you do out of habit, and without question, that might prevent your success in life, love and business?"
- 武 When was the last time you consciously chose to question your habits, beliefs, and actions?"

Unless you begin questioning the validity and reasoning behind your beliefs and habits, you will almost certainly miss many of life's golden opportunities.

Changing Self-Limiting Beliefs

There are many self-limiting beliefs. At some time during your life, you have probably asked yourself one or more of the following questions via your self-talk: "Why is X more successful than I am at either A, B or C?" I am also confident that your reply, via your self-talk mechanism, was like one of the following answers:

- "They have family money, so life and business are easier for them."
- "They have better connections than I do."
- "They are just luckier than I am."
- "They are much cleverer than I am."
- "They are naturally slim, and I can't lose weight."
- "They have got a natural sense of timekeeping; I am never on time."
- "They are always in control; I am simply no good with money."
- "They are naturally gifted; I am just not a good driver."

Do any of these seem vaguely familiar? Naturally, your questions and answers may have been phrased slightly differently; however, the answers will probably be the same. You may even begin making excuses to mask the truth. Taking the axiom that I have already discussed, in that our perceptions and beliefs will eventually become our version of reality, then by making such excuses, you are only serving to reinforce your own self-limiting beliefs.

More importantly, if you do not act to change your negative belief system into something positive, you will reinforce a growing number of negative beliefs. Even worse, you could develop a victim mentality that may stay with you for the remainder of your life. How do you change self-limiting, negative beliefs? The process is surprisingly simple. In fact, it is almost too simple, which causes some people to initially doubt its effectiveness. I cannot stress strongly enough that you should not doubt it whatsoever; the technique I will describe works exceedingly well.

To change or modify self-limiting beliefs into a more positive belief pattern, you must simply learn how to caveat. In other words, you need to add a positive qualification to your negative self-talk statements. This caveat technique is amazingly effective, and it allows positive changes to begin taking effect from the moment you start using it. When you start to caveat a negative self-talk statement, you immediately begin to positively reprogram your thought patterns, together with your related belief systems. Using this technique, the change from negative to positive core beliefs will be almost effortless and virtually unnoticed. On occasion, it might even be fun! Once you add a suitable caveat, the previous list will look slightly different. Here are some suggested caveats that change the previously negative statements into positive ones.

- "They have family money, so life and business are easier for them." – **Caveat** – "But, my income is increasing, and I will reach my target independently."
- "They have better connections than I do." – **Caveat** – "But I am lucky in the connections I do have, and I am making new and better ones all the time."
- "They are just luckier than I am." – **Caveat** – "'But you can make your luck; I am already really lucky, and getting luckier every day."
- "They are much cleverer than I am." – **Caveat** – "But I am really smart too, and in many other ways. A particular paper qualification does not necessarily make someone smarter; it just means they've passed an exam, which anyone can do if they study for it."
- "They are naturally slim, and I cannot lose weight." – **Caveat** – "But now I have modified my lifestyle with healthier eating and exercise. Things will soon change, and I will look and feel amazing soon."

- 武 "They have a natural sense of time keeping; I am never on time." - **Caveat**: - "But I am getting better every day."
- 武 "They are always in control; I am simply no good with money." – **Caveat** – "But I am taking control, and all will be well."
- 武 "They are naturally gifted; I have never been a good driver." – **Caveat** – "But with practice, I soon will be."

As you can see, adding a simple caveat is not difficult. More importantly, once you get into the habit of adding a caveat when you find yourself making a negative remark via your self-talk, your positive response mechanism will begin to protect you automatically. No matter what your caveat might be—a couple of words or even a whole sentence—it should always be positive and realistic.

To caveat with what you know to be unrealistic or even with an untruth is highly unwise. For example, if you were to allow your self-talk to become negative concerning your poor earnings, then a caveat statement such as "But I will be a millionaire soon" would be ridiculous. This would be extremely damaging unless it were true and realistically within your reach. Instead, a better caveat might be: "But my earnings are improving, and my wealth is steadily increasing."

I strongly urge you to try the caveat technique for a minimum of 21 days because you will experience the dramatic difference it makes. Remember that after just 21 days of doing something, you will have formed a new, more positive habit. You will also have unleashed a ripple effect of other extremely positive long-term changes.

Third-Party Belief

Third-party belief is extremely important because it is how the people you interact with perceive you. In other words, it is your image and credibility to the outside world. The precise definition of credibility refers to both the subjective and objective components of believability. Building third-party belief in your credibility requires two key elements. The first is your expertise in what you do, and the second is your trustworthiness. For others to have complete belief in you, making you credible to them in every way, there should be no conflicting messages. For example, a conflicting message might be created in the following way.

In this scenario, I work for a company selling insurance and attend a sales appointment to sell my products to a large corporation. Naturally, I wish to project the image that I am successful and good at my job and climbing the corporate ladder of success. However, I attended the meeting wearing a cheap, ill-fitting suit, I wore old shoes which were scuffed and repaired, and I used free hotel pens and notepaper carried in a shoddy briefcase. What message would I be projecting, and what beliefs would the people I meet with begin to form about me? The messages I project would undoubtedly suggest that I was not successful at all. They may even suggest that I might struggle to hold down a job. My appearance would create a conflict of credibility in the minds of others. Therefore, even if I make an excellent sales presentation at the meeting, I probably will not win the business, no matter how hard I try.

To ensure that you create a positive third-party belief in others and ensure your credibility remains intact, you should ensure there are no conflicting messages in the image you project. Every detail about you combines to create a greater whole, reinforcing whatever message you wish to convey. Without third-party belief and credibility, others will not fully believe in your trustworthiness, professional abilities, or expertise.

Self-Talk

Your self-talk, or inner monologue, is your voice, expressed only in your mind as you think and process thoughts. Every thought and conversation we have in our minds is either neutral, positive, or negative. The deciding factor is you. Remember that we each choose how we perceive all things in our world. Therefore, we all decide what is good or bad concerning ourselves and how we feel. Even the great William Shakespeare wrote: "There is nothing either good or bad, but thinking makes it so." Everything we receive as input into our mind is technically nothing more than raw data, which is then processed so that we can decide how we wish to categorise it.

Therefore, through self-talk, we can brainwash ourselves into believing any reality our self-talk conditions us to believe. For example, when your self-talk says, "I always do that," or "I can never do that," you are conditioning your mind to that belief. With repeated self-talk reinforcement of that same message, your suggested belief eventually becomes your new reality. However, your self-talk can be both your greatest ally and your worst enemy. Negative self-talk can damage your business potential and limit your personal growth. Conversely, positive self-talk can be your key to releasing your full potential. It is entirely your choice which one.

Effective Visualisation

Visualisation creates a perfect scenario in your mind that comprises all the sensory input that a real scenario would provide. Once this state has been achieved, you can mentally rehearse a multitude of action and response scenarios. However, it is essential to visualise all the processes required to reach your desired targets, not simply the result.

It is important to remember that there is a huge difference between visualisation and fantasy. Never confuse the two. For example, since I became an international martial arts coach, I got to know many fighters who have used visualisation techniques before a big fight. Unfortunately, most would only visualise winning the fight, and once they were in the ring, they would usually find the actual winning process vastly different. The winners typically visualise a realistic and detailed plan, allowing for changes and injury. Without these essential elements, they would be more in fantasy than effective visualisation.

Effective visualisation is an excellent way to make your objectives more tangible and achievable. All top athletes are coached using effective visualisation techniques to help give them an edge in competition. It takes them from being relatively nebulous and ethereal to becoming far more substantive. During any visualisation process, I suggest you also explore some of your deep desires and initial core responses to those feelings.

Visualisation involves placing yourself in a dream-like state and then imagining all the details that comprise your target and how to reach it. Even if you are sceptical about the technique, please try it for yourself because it works. Your mind is structured to make it work effectively like this. Different people might visualise in different ways, but if done properly, they all work well. I visualise it as if I were watching a movie about whatever I am focusing on.

This is probably because I have been heavily involved in the TV and movie business over the years. Other people immerse themselves in visualisation in different sensory ways, which is usually dependent upon whatever their preferred communication bias might be. Visualisation works best when you relax and let go of all your conscious thoughts. Then, let your feelings work for you to get what you want. A place for effective visualisation should be somewhere quiet and without interruption. Here are the steps which will help you achieve a state of effective visualisation:

- 武 Envision the appropriate environment according to your desired target.
- 武 Imagine that you can view yourself performing the skill or in that state of being as if you are looking through a movie camera. This camera will view you as an audience would, and it might be moving slowly towards you, as it allows the viewer to pick up every detail of the scene. This camera will pick up the lighting, the sounds, and even the different scents of the scenario. The more detail you can visualise, the better it will be.
- 武 Now, change to the viewer's perspective. This is a multi-dimensional visualisation, where you can be both the viewer and the subject at the same time. Now, you have become the subject performing the desired skill or in the desired state of being. Add as much detail to the envisioned scenario as possible.

- 武 Add a wildcard. This is not normally included in suggested visualisation techniques; however, I believe it to be extremely important. The wildcard should be that something has suddenly affected your perfect visualisation, forcing you to compensate, improvise, and then change the plan to achieve your desired objectives.
- 武 Concluding the visualisation is where the visualised scenario returns to the reality of where you are now. Once again, just like in a scene from a movie, you can shift from being the subject to becoming the viewing audience at will. In doing so, the concluding scene might become the reverse of the opening scene, with the camera pulling back to the overview shot before dissolving back into reality.
- 武 The more intricate detail you create while visualising, the more it will strengthen the pathways in your mind that allow you to perform those skills or to reach the desired state. Your brain does not recognise much difference between the real thing and a complex, detailed, and complete visualisation, which is the main reason why visualisation is so effective.
- 武 The next step would be to apply the visualisation in different and broader ways. For example, perhaps envision what it might feel like for you to A) Feel extremely successful. B) Feel extremely wealthy. C) Feel extremely healthy and fit.

Your list of desires can naturally include whatever you want. The important thing is that you relate to them. Try to hold the mental image of positive energy for as long as possible and without interruption. I suggest you examine in detail the qualities and attributes your visualised environment might possess. If you ever find doubt, fear, or negativity entering your mind, then remember the positive things in your life. Never forget that fear creates the victim; you are not a victim.

Natural Mental Martial Artists

Many famous people throughout history have used the principles of my system of mental martial arts without realising it. Such people seem to instinctively know precisely what to do to communicate well and connect with those around them. Such people always seem to bring harmony where there was formerly discord. These gifted individuals have proven themselves, time and again, to be incredible negotiators, capable of producing win-win solutions to seemingly impossible problems. Observing these 'natural Mental Martial Artists' in action or reading about their achievements is always a source of inspiration. These individuals have a remarkable ability to align their energy with others and seamlessly blend in, gaining control of any situation. Who are these individuals? While I could list many, I'll mention just a few, confident that you'll be able to think of numerous other examples yourself.

Some naturally gifted Mental Martial Artists:

- Former British Prime Minister Sir Winston Churchill.
- The former Governor of California and the world's greatest-ever bodybuilder, Arnold Schwarzenegger.
- The greatest athlete of the 20th century and the greatest boxer of all time, Muhammad Ali.
- The incredible Martin Luther King, Jr.
- Former President of the Soviet Union, Mikhail Gorbachev.
- Former US President Ronald Reagan.
- Former US President Abraham Lincoln.
- The wonderfully inspirational Zig Ziglar.
- Former British Prime Minister Margaret Thatcher.
- Author, composer and moviemaker Cliff Twemlow.

Chapter 3 Summary – Power Moves:

- *'**Who Dares Wins'**—The motto of the British SAS Regiment is also an excellent personal mantra.*
- *Flexibility will keep you standing in the face of the storm, whereas the rigid and inflexible will break.*

- 武 Nothing is stronger or weaker, better or worse – only different.
- 武 It is better to win a war by not having one.
- 武 Your beliefs create energy, which can lead to better luck, business success, good health, and true love. It will make your vision of the good life a reality.
- 武 You create your reality because your perception is always your reality.

Chapter 3 Summary – Pressure Points:

- 武 Make change your friend.
- 武 Never accuse anyone of your imagination.
- 武 Flexibility is the key to success; even the mightiest tree may be blown down by the wind, while a humble blade of grass will remain standing.
- 武 When your preparation meets with suitable opportunities, success will naturally occur.
- 武 There is no such thing as failure.
- 武 Only you choose how you see things.
- 武 Logic will not change an emotion, but action will.
- 武 Never confuse activity with accomplishment.
- 武 Never draw a universe from a single word, deed, or action.
- 武 Understand the difference between reaction and response.
- 武 You can reprogram your mind.
- 武 Learn to caveat a negative thought or word with a positive statement.
- 武 Learn how to question your beliefs, your belief patterns, and those of others.

Chapter 4: Mental Martial Arts Mind

Regardless of your pursuits, always strive to give your best. Moreover, aim to understand your chosen fields so deeply that you can teach them. This level of mastery not only allows you to share your knowledge but also reveals the vastness of what you have yet to learn.

Consider the misconception many beginners in physical martial arts hold. They often believe that earning a Black Belt signifies the pinnacle of knowledge in the art. This belief is far from the truth. In reality, it's only after achieving this milestone that true learning begins. The journey to mastery is a continuous process, and even with a Black Belt, one is still a relative beginner.

As a novice at anything, you must think consciously about everything you do, every move involved, and every process in the execution chain. At the beginner stage, you will appear clumsy, slow, and awkward at whatever you are attempting to do. However, with time and practice, you soon shift the process away from your conscious mind and into your subconscious. At this stage, you hardly notice yourself performing the techniques, let alone thinking consciously about how to accomplish them. You can just do them.

An excellent example of this process, which I am sure everyone can relate to, is when you first learn how to drive a car. Your goal as a beginner was to gain your driver's license and, in doing so, become a legal driver. I am sure you remember some of the many mistakes you made during the learning process and how you had to concentrate hard even when performing what was a comparatively simple manoeuvre. If you learned to drive in a car with a manual transmission, as I did, you may also remember the times you caused the gears to grind when you did not quite change correctly when depressing the clutch. Even worse is the number of times you stalled the car because you let the clutch out too fast while simultaneously depressing the gas pedal.

However, with considerable practice, you could soon concentrate less on the physical processes of operating the car and more on your roadcraft techniques. With even more practice, you eventually reached the point where you could get into any vehicle and drive it immediately without thinking twice about any physical processes involved. More importantly, I am sure that everyone who has passed their driver's test will agree with me when I say that the action of passing your test does not automatically make you a good driver. You only learned how to become a good driver once you had passed your test. Therefore, to become good or even an expert at something, including my system of Mental Martial Arts, you need to take the following steps:

- You first learn and understand the basics.
- You practice the basics.
- You become completely conversant with the basics and with all other related skills. Instead of consciously thinking about the physical actions required to perform skills, you perform them automatically without conscious thought.

Shifting processes from the conscious mind into the subconscious mind takes place in the following stages:

- Before you started to read this book, you probably had no idea that my system of Mental Martial Arts existed.
- Without that knowledge, you would be unable to practice it.
- You then learned of its existence and bought this book. This made you aware of the subject.
- In the beginning, when practising Mental Martial Arts, you are conscious of the skills required to perform the techniques.
- However, since Mental Martial Arts are still new to you, it is not easy to apply them in practice.
- With practice over time, you become increasingly competent at performing the skills.
- During practice, the processes and skills required to perform Mental Martial Arts eventually shift from the conscious mind to the subconscious mind.

- 武 Eventually, you do not have to consciously think about how to perform the techniques; you can just do them. As a result, the speed of your mastery of those techniques also increases.
- 武 With even more practice, you eventually gain what is known as subconscious mastery of the art. At this point, you are ready to start teaching others how to perform my system of Mental Martial Arts.

Multi-Dimensional Thinking

To explain what I mean by multi-dimensional thinking, I will begin by clarifying what two-dimensional linear thinking is. Linear thinking could be the process of logical thought in progression, where a specific response to a step must first be obtained before another step is taken.

Therefore, non-linear multidimensional thinking could be the expansion of both thought and logic in multiple dimensions, as opposed to a single direction. It involves concepts with multiple starts and endpoints to which logic can be applied to produce different outcomes. Non-linear multi-dimensional thought processes greatly increase the number of potential outcomes for any concept. This technique provides a distinct advantage to any individual or business.

Someone who can envision and think in multidimensional ways will probably be able to anticipate events and situations as metaphoric multidimensional dots. They would then begin to make connections with the metaphoric dots in non-linear ways across different dimensions. Using this technique, they could quickly envision multiple possible outcomes to any event, problem, or situation.

To a certain degree, such conceptual thinkers are naturally gifted with this ability. The good news for those not naturally gifted with this ability is that it can be learned. With practice, learning this technique and developing the ability to envision multiple outcomes is possible. People who open their minds to the possibility of new things and are relaxed and flexible will eventually be able to imagine new and creative opportunities.

To help make the process easier, it is essential to never dismiss even supposedly wild ideas without carefully considering them. Not every wild idea will have merit; however, some will undoubtedly do. In short, you should never forget to dare to dream.

Creative, Lateral Thinking

Creative, or lateral thinking, is used to find solutions to problems through nonlinear, nontraditional, and innovative approaches. This begs the question: if creative, lateral thinking is about nonlinear reasoning, which produces ideas that are usually not obtainable by traditional methods, can the process be taught and learned? The answer to this critical question is still unclear because some people have more of a natural aptitude for creativity than others. However, it does seem possible to coach people to become more creative than they were previously.

Most people have been brainwashed from an early age into taking a linear approach to life. Most businesses demand it, and in fact, modern Western education systems seem to be structured in a way that perpetuates this. I believe that to succeed more easily in life, love, and business, a more creatively lateral approach should always be sought and considered.

For example, in the Western U.S. K-12 education system, a revolution began when Professor Eric Mazur at Harvard University started pioneering work on what has now become known as the Flipped Classroom teaching method. After it developed into a complete teaching model, it was given a huge launch in 2012 at the Tribeca Media Arts Academy in Chicago to education leaders and the public. The visionary educational thought leader, Thomas Lapping, of Eduvision and JDL Horizons, was responsible for that launch. In doing so, he helped lead the way to revolutionise K-12 education for the 21st century. I am also proud to call Tom a close friend.

Did creative, lateral thinking have a vital role in the proliferation of the Flipped Classroom and its conception? Absolutely! Without Tom Lapping's wonderfully imaginative, lateral-thinking mind to launch the concept in the way he did, I believe that the concept may have remained nothing more than an interesting idea adopted by only a few schools. In my opinion, Tom's creative thinking in the way the idea was launched in Chicago was the driving force behind the Flipped Classroom model becoming widely adopted.

I will briefly overview the Flipped Classroom concept and, in doing so, demonstrate how creative, lateral thinking flipped teaching methods turned traditional methods upside down. Using this model as opposed to the traditional 'sage on the stage' classroom model, there is a fundamental difference in roles and techniques. In the Flipped Classroom model, the role is changed for both teachers and students. There has also been a fundamental change in how information is disseminated and how and when students perform their studies. The Flipped Classroom approach to teaching reverses homework and classroom teaching roles.

We were all taught at school that the traditional teaching method is for students to have classroom lectures. During these lectures, the teacher explains a topic, which is usually followed by homework.

In the Flipped Classroom model, the student first studies the topic alone, typically using video or other digital/cyber mediums. The student attempts to apply their newfound knowledge in the classroom by doing practical work. This often involves working in small groups using project-based learning techniques or one-to-one coaching with the teacher. Therefore, the classroom teacher's role is flipped, and the initial data is no longer imparted in a lecture format. Instead, the teacher's role is that of a coach. They mentor the students when they need help, but only after students have initially studied the subject alone.

The use of readily available modern technology, such as tablets, smartphones, video, and DVD players, has helped to make this quantum shift possible. However, the critical point is that creative and lateral thinking is required to question the existing teaching model, hypothesise, model a new concept, and then implement a revolutionary new approach to teaching.

This is a particularly remarkable achievement for educators because they are part of what is often wrongly seen as a slow-to-innovate and linear-thinking institution. Tom Lapping's vision and lateral thinking launched the concept to 'centre stage' in a spectacular way, helping to make it a widely accepted practice.

The Jeet Kune Do of Lateral Thinking and Learning

Jeet Kune Do is the martial arts style that the amazing Bruce Lee developed. However, I believe that the term 'Jeet Kune Do' is more than just a name suitable for a martial arts style; it represents the epitome of lateral thinking. Bruce Lee devised a style of combat that eliminated what he termed 'the classical mess.' He considered it essential to reinvent the traditional, rigid fighting styles. He thought that rigid, fixed styles had to evolve, or they would eventually become extinct.

The same is true in life, love, and business. They either evolve or eventually become extinct. In business, the traditional, rigid, fixed pattern thinking usually prevents and restricts what it seeks to achieve. Those in positions of power and leadership who are not strong and courageous in this respect need to step aside and let progress happen naturally. If they do not, they will eventually be embarrassingly eliminated as economic and corporate natural selection removes them. Traditional, rigid, fixed-pattern leadership does not simply help to prevent progress; it can completely kill it. They can even kill nations.

Just as Jeet Kune Do was developed into the art of fighting without fighting, companies need to create the art of doing business without doing business in the traditional sense. Modern businesses can no longer afford to remain under a fixed-pattern system. Creativity should flow as an expression of both the leadership and the overall expression of the organisation. Bruce Lee taught his students to: "Be like water, move fluidly, and without hesitation." I call this Fluid Force.

SCALI

I use an acronym to describe what might be considered the epitome of improvisational creative lateral thinking. It also describes the thought processes behind it. The acronym I use is S.C.A.L.I. which is pronounced 'scally' as in the word scallywag, or 'skah lee' depending upon your English dialect. This acronym stands for:

- 武 Sub-Conscious
- 武 Applied
- 武 Lateral
- 武 Improvisational (thinking)

I derived the acronym S.C.A.L.I. from a nickname common in Northwest England. The nickname describes a subculture of people who live daily by their wits. These people do not always follow the more traditional courses in life that society, in general, would almost certainly prefer. Therefore, my term S.C.A.L.I. is an abbreviated adaptation of the term scallywag, derived from an old Irish word, sgaileog, meaning to drudge or be a farm servant.

While working with BBC TV News, I witnessed many times how these people are excellent at finding some of the most creative ways to live and do business outside and around the traditional system. They also find the most innovative and creative ways to circumvent even the strictest rules laid out by society to carry out their alternative way of doing business. These people are some of the most innovative, lateral thinkers around.

When I have coached my system of Mental Martial Arts to large corporations I have often been included as a guest coach at some of their team-building events. One such event took place in the English Lake District. It involved a multi-national pharmaceutical company that had funded a program to help rehabilitate young offenders, or scallywags, back into society.

These young offenders perfectly fit my S.C.A.L.I. profile, so I was curious to learn how they would perform in the team-building exercises against some of the brightest academic minds on Earth. During the two-day team-building course, the S.C.A.L.I. team was in direct competition with the corporate team of senior executives, doctors, and scientists. The S.C.A.L.I. team consisted of people who had barely finished school, with even the most basic qualifications. Naturally, those who devised the event thought that the corporate team would lead the way and set an example for the S.C.A.L.I. team to follow. They also thought that the corporate team would teach the S.C.A.L.I. team how the application of science by those with a first-class education would help them overcome the obstacles and surprises awaiting them during the intense two-day course. How completely wrong they were.

From the beginning, the S.C.A.L.I. team demonstrated exceptional lateral thinking skills, and the outcome at every stage of the team-building exercises was always the same. The S.C.A.L.I. team comprehensively beat the corporate team every time, and they clearly demonstrated superior abilities in creative lateral thinking in all exercises. These exercises included efficiently and effectively gathering tools and supplies and devising innovative ways to cross rivers with only a few basic tools, such as rope and wood. At the end of the two-day course, the competition results were a complete embarrassment for the corporate team of academics because they lost in every event. Therefore, there are several $64,000 questions which are:

- "Can scallywags be made into respectable business people and thought leaders?"
- "Could the essence of lateral, creative S.C.A.L.I. thinking be analysed, quantified, and formalised in a way which could then be taught to others?"
- "Would the process of formalising and quantifying S.C.A.L.I. thinking into a structured system neutralise the important essence of that thinking?"

An important 1st step would be to make emotional contact with and engage with these exceptionally gifted people. In doing so, perhaps it might motivate them more positively regarding their societal role. Learning how to harness their creative essence and apply it in the business world might eventually become possible. Another possibility is to create teams of S.C.A.L.I. thinkers and those who have been trained in a traditional linear system so that each might learn from the other and work together. I imagine that this would almost certainly help linear thinkers become more creative and lateral S.C.A.L.I. thinkers become more useful in a corporate environment.

I do not know the answer at this point. However, the fact remains that S.C.A.L.I. thinking gets results and gets them fast. The senior management of the pharmaceutical company that produced the team-building event should have considered how they might harness the newfound creative power they witnessed in action. Perhaps they did. However, I suspect that even if they did at least question the possibility of attempting to harness that new creative force, it was probably then lost somewhere in a corporate in-tray.

The good news is that some people are natural S.C.A.L.I. thinkers without being real scallywags by social definition. These people are responsible members of society and are outstanding businesspeople and famous entrepreneurs. This also begs the question, "Why are there not more S.C.A.L.I. thinkers in senior corporate positions?" I believe that this is probably because both business and academia have traditionally mistakenly revered the linear mind. Traditional academic institutions typically produce two hugely different types of graduates. Some are entrepreneur material, becoming stars of the business world. The next group are intelligent but lacks basic common sense. They cannot simply apply their academic knowledge in the real world. Another reason why S.C.A.L.I. thinkers are not more commonly found in corporate entities is that they typically enjoy greater freedom to produce and create independently. This greater degree of freedom is usually only afforded by self-employment, often in small and extraordinarily successful small businesses. These people typically lead the organisations they create, allowing the linear thinkers to perform all daily operations.

Thankfully, there seems to be a shift taking place that is heralding the dawn of a new era in business. The proverbial keys to the kingdom of corporate power are slowly changing hands from the traditional linear thinkers to the creative lateral thinkers. An increasing number of leaders think in S.C.A.L.I. style at all levels, both in the corporate world and in the government. Such people have a definite left-brain-right-brain intermix, resulting in a new kind of balanced thinker. Such thinkers possess the traditionally revered linear qualities in combination with an exceptionally creative, lateral thinking talent.

Left-Brain, Right-Brain

The concept of there being a differential between left-brain and right-brain thinking is far from new. It was developed from early 20th-century research, which discovered that the two sides of the human brain have two quite different and distinct ways of thinking. The left brain processes data in a predominantly analytical, linear fashion, whereas the right brain processes data in a more conceptual, visual, and simultaneous manner.

I remember one of my lecturers at university gave me a valuable tip to help me detect if someone is left or right-brain dominant. She suggested that I look for obvious signs of right-brain dominant people because they are usually 'hand-talkers,' or people who gesture with their hands a great deal when they talk. She also suggested looking for other signs, such as people who do not usually read instruction manuals. These are both typically excellent indicators of right-brain dominant people, with the reverse being true for those who are left-brain dominant.

Interestingly, many people mistakenly believe that left-handed people are right-brain dominant, but this is not the case. There is currently no known correlation between brain dominance and hand dominance. What does all this mean in more practical terms? How can you identify and understand the difference between the two kinds of thinking? I have prepared a short comparison chart to help you understand this concept fully. This chart clearly describes the differences between those who are left-brain dominant and those who are right-brain dominant. Understanding these differentials will help you detect and maximise the strengths of such people within your organisation. It also gives the Mental Martial Artist valuable intelligence about how someone processes information. This is an excellent indicator of what kind of opponent they will be. The better you understand your opponent, the easier it will be to gain control of an engagement and help you reach your desired outcome.

Right-Brain	**Left-Brain**
Tend to lack organisation.	Tend to be highly organised.
Tend to process ideas simultaneously.	Tend to process ideas in sequence.
Highly unlikely to read instruction manuals or charts.	Highly likely to read instruction manuals or charts.
Tend to envision a greater 'whole' rather than the parts and the details.	They tend to look at parts rather than the 'whole' as they progress towards the target while being focused on detail in a sequential manner.

Make rapid lateral connections.	Make logical deductions.
They like to know the reasons 'why' rules exist.	Likely to follow rules without questioning.
Usually, do not plan	Usually, plan and make lists.
Random in nature	Logical and linear in nature.
Led more by feelings and intuition.	Led more by logic and reasoning.
Possessing a free-flowing, fluid mindset	Possessing an analytical mindset
Tend to be subjective.	Tend to be objective.
Tend to be tactile.	Tend to be observational.
Tend to prioritise poorly.	Tend to plan ahead.
Usually, talk using hand gestures.	Rarely, if ever, talk with hand gestures.
Visually and image-focused.	Usually focused on data, words, and numbers.
At ease with change.	Cautious of change.
Usually, have little or no sense of time.	They are typically good at keeping time.
Use mind maps, mind pictures and mind illustrations to remember things.	Usually, use data, objects, symbols, or words to remember things.

Chapter 4 Summary – Power Move:

武   Achieving a 'Black Belt' in mental martial arts requires study and commitment.

Chapter 4 Summary – Pressure Points:

武   Value creative, lateral thinking.

武   Make better decisions by using both the right and the left sides of your brain.

Chapter 5: Communication

"A good speech should be like a woman's skirt: long enough to cover the subject and short enough to create interest."

Sir Winston Churchill

The quote above by Sir Winston Churchill says everything about communication in one sentence. Good communication skills are vital to your success. Everyone needs to learn to convey messages smoothly, thoroughly, and succinctly. Words are powerful. Therefore, optimum communication skills are essential at every level of human interaction.

Good communication makes the business world function or fail, and is also the substance on which our most intimate personal relationships are built. It should not surprise anyone that poor communication is crucial to why business and personal relationships can break down and fail. Good communication skills are vital in life, love, and business.

Let us take a closer look at communication. Communication is the process of conveying information. This takes three primary forms: words, body language or nonverbal communication, and graphics. For our purposes, we are not including the graphic form of communication as it is irrelevant at this juncture. The basis of all communication is that the medium, or the language of our communication, must be clearly understood by both parties to be effective.

Most people usually forget that what they are trying to communicate to others must be received by them so that they can fully understand it. If the receiver does not understand what is being said, it is a complete waste of time and effort. You may think that you are making yourself clear; however, if the listener is not receiving you, you may as well be reading from a Chinese railway timetable using the Greek language to a person who only speaks Dutch.

If used positively, verbal communication can glorify humanity, build nations, and even express your deepest love for another person. If used negatively, words can hurt beyond reason. They can even destroy nations just as easily as they can destroy personal relationships. I will loosely paraphrase the great English author, poet, and philosopher Geoffrey Chaucer: "Words can obliterate a person for eternity."

You have probably heard your parents or grandparents wisely inform you that many people "talk a lot but say very little." This is quite common, and it is wise to avoid doing this yourself. When you detect this trait in a person you are communicating with, you should take the lead and endeavour to keep the conversation on track. Encourage them to be concise by politely cutting off avenues for them to ramble on about nothing of any real significance.

Naturally, it would be best if you always communicated with others from a position of absolute integrity. As a person of honour, you should always say what you mean and mean what you say. These factors should be the bedrock of all your communications. Furthermore, I strongly urge you to always speak positively about others and never speak negatively about anyone or anything.

Generally, if you wish positive things to be said about you, always speaking positively about others is a good idea. Since words have great power, choose and use your words very carefully. In many ways, words can be just as powerful as any physical weapon, and in some ways more so. Therefore, treat your words with great respect, just as you would a gun or a knife.

Words can be confusing at times, and certain words may mean one thing to you while at the same time meaning something entirely different to someone else. For example, the words vision and sight technically have the same meaning. However, if a man says to his wife or girlfriend, "Honey, you're a vision," it would be a great compliment. Alternatively, if the same man chose to say, "Honey, you look a sight," it would be taken as a huge insult. However, if you said to that person they were "a sight for sore eyes," then your message would revert to becoming a compliment once again. Such is the power of the simple word choices we make daily using English.

Vocabulary

There are estimated to be between 500,000 and 1,000,000 words in the English language, with new words being added daily. Surprisingly, research indicates that an average adult who uses English as a first language will only understand somewhere between 50,000 and 250,000 words. Some people have a command of extensive vocabulary, and these people are typically great orators. One such person who was also arguably the greatest statesman of all time, Sir Winston Churchill, was reputed to have a vocabulary in the region of 400,000 words! The great William Shakespeare has been estimated to have used only about 29,500 words in his collective literary works. Therefore, it could be estimated that his vocabulary was in the region of 295,000 words. In more common day-to-day life, most people probably only use about 10% of the total words within their entire vocabulary. Ipso facto, someone who understands 50,000 words will probably only use around 5,000 in daily conversation.

The greater your vocabulary range, the better prepared you are to engage any opponent in conversation at any level of life, love, and business. I deliberately chose to use the phrase ipso facto in the last paragraph to help me make a serious point. I urge you all, especially those speaking English as a first language, to better understand Latin. This is one of the basic foundations of language. A basic understanding of Latin will also give you much pleasure in understanding the root and meaning of many of the words you use daily.

Communication Combinations

In my concept of Mental Martial Arts, verbal and non-verbal communication from your opponent typically provides all the clues you need to conclude an engagement satisfactorily. These vital communication clues will also enable you to formulate the appropriate strategies, tactics, and responses to blend with, align with, and redirect your opponent's energy. Since the overall target of any possible conflict is always to win a war by not having it, the better you are in terms of your communication skills, the better you will be at achieving that objective.

The rules for engaging a single person and group communication are virtually identical. However, just as when engaging multiple attackers in the physical martial arts, a little more experience and training are required when engaging multiple opponents simultaneously.

Any form of direct engagement and stressful situations usually generate intense emotions in those involved. In such circumstances, rational thinking on your opponent's part is typically the engagement's first casualty. It is essential always to use clear and strategic communication. During intense and emotional engagements, you should always aim to minimise the possibility that unwelcome distractions may occur. This will maximise the chance of both you and your opponent remaining focused on the engagement and of you achieving a successful outcome. While in an engagement, staying objective is always best, and you should never make any of it personal. To help you avoid this pitfall, stick to the facts and remain as dispassionate, calm, and focused as possible. Taking this may even help you reach a conclusion where all parties involved feel as if they've each gained a victory somehow.

Speak Well

Practice developing a well-rounded, confident, and commanding voice. Always use good vocabulary and clear diction because this will go a long way towards improving your overall appearance. In turn, this will also subconsciously help to improve your overall self-confidence. Deliberately speak less than you usually do in a social situation with close family or friends. However, when you speak, do so clearly and make yourself heard. Never fear public speaking. Instead, learn to embrace the opportunity. Any reservations and fears you may have about this are probably the same as those of the person next to you, so you are usually never alone, and everyone feels similarly. When you speak in public, speak up for yourself confidently, and you will find that your audience will be much more impressed than you think. When performing public speaking, always try to do so more slowly than in general daily conversation. Make your points succinctly and clearly when in a meeting or while giving a presentation. This will create a positive, lasting impression about you in the minds of both your peers and your bosses. Learning the art of genuinely complimenting and praising others is also a good idea. It is also essential to learn how to receive a compliment graciously.

Communication Tips

Here are some tips which will help to maximise your overall success in all types of communication.

- 武 Do not automatically expect everyone to like you. Remove your ego from the equation and communicate clearly.
- 武 Always control the pace of your communication. Your voice should have a calm tone, an undulating pitch, and a confident delivery.
- 武 Your voice should be able to control the conversation, which is one reason why you should always avoid talking too fast. Talking too fast might suggest to others that you are nervous, too eager, or simply inexperienced. Using a deliberately slower and calmer pace suggests confidence and control, which is a quality people will usually gravitate towards.
- 武 Always try to avoid raising your voice. People who are naturally powerful and who possess a great presence do not need to do that.
- 武 Once you have said what you intended to say and made your point, leave it there. Do not talk too much, no matter how tempting this option may seem. Doing so will only dilute the

power of what you have already said and the perception of your overall power and presence.
- Do not be too concerned if others do not keep up with you during the conversation engagement. Nor should you worry about the time it takes for others to fully understand what you have said. Powerful people do not let this concern them.
- In physical martial arts, the eye line between you and your opponent is important. The same is true in Mental Martial Arts and all personal face-to-face communication.
- It is also a good idea to practice looking very slightly above the eye line of your opponent. Doing this has the effect of conveying a slight hint of your superiority without saying anything. The military makes use of this technique very effectively. Take note of the low peaked caps of the drill sergeants. These are designed to rest down over the eyes, which forces the wearer to hold their head high and slightly back. In assuming this position, the wearer will have to look down on those with whom they are communicating. This is a nonverbal signal of superiority, which is further emphasised by an appropriate tone of voice. However, you should be careful not to hold your head and eye line at a level that is too high. If you do so, you will simply appear arrogant, snooty, and even downright silly.
- If you are thrust into social or business situations where others are more knowledgeable than you are about a specific topic, then guide the flow of conversation onto a topic that you know well. In these types of situations, always carefully respond to questions you would prefer not to answer. Step out of the energy line of the question and generally respond by asking challenging questions in return. You might even wish to guide those questions on a slight tangent to the original question, which was directed to you. If you wish to move the conversation in a different direction, then wait until you can pick up on a point that offers a natural diversion to another topic.
- It is a good habit to use the summary tactic during meetings and important conversations, which paraphrases what has been said.

This not only clarifies matters to all parties, but it also has the effect of making it appear that you are listening keenly and that you are deeply knowledgeable.

- 武 Always try to avoid competing in areas where you are simply out of your depth. If you do so, then you are likely to come unstuck in a big way. The same would happen if a physical martial artist were to go into combat against a much more powerful and skilled opponent.
- 武 In general, you should always endeavour to take the lead. As you do so, you can control and lift the pace, humour, and enthusiasm of the conversation. This is especially important if you detect that the conversation is becoming too sombre. Conversely, if the company is a little too high, then you should endeavour to take the lead and become the calming voice of confidence and wisdom.
- 武 You should avoid talking over people. If you ever sense yourself doing this, then rein yourself back at all costs. Talking over people sends the message that you do not care what others say, and it is simply extremely rude to do so. If you wish to make a point or to interject, then always wait for an appropriate break in the conversation.
- 武 During a conversation, always give your opponent your undivided attention. Learn to become a good listener. If someone cuts across you while you are speaking, never be swayed. Simply continue with what you are saying undeterred. Maintain your pace, tone, and level of calmness. This will send a non-verbal message for them to back off, especially if supported with a non-verbal communication signal such as a knowing look.
- 武 Focus on the quality of what you say, not how much you say. Powerful people usually say extraordinarily little. When they say something, it generally has an impact.
- 武 If you take notes during a conversation, it may suggest that you are finding some useful gems of information in what is being

communicated. However, you should be aware that if you make constant notes, then you may appear to be more like a secretary rather than a business counterpart.

Communication Clues

In Mental Martial Arts, automatically looking for vital signs, signals, and biases in your opponent's conversation is always a good idea. This will help you identify exactly how your opponent best receives and processes information.

Once you understand this about your opponent, whatever you communicate to them will always have a more significant impact. This can even make the difference between being heard, understood, and considered seriously or being dismissed because your words are not getting through! Word clues are the signs, signals, and biases you should look for during conversations. These word clues will all fall into one or more of the following categories:

- 武 **V**isual
- 武 **A**udible
- 武 **T**actile or Kinaesthetic
- 武 **O**lfactory or Gustatory
- 武 **D**ata or Digital

Once you have identified specific word clues and biases in your opponent's communication, you will typically begin to see a pattern forming. These patterns might be easier to spot with some people compared to others. However, there will always be a pattern, so you need to be observant and persistent until you identify it. When you have identified your opponent's preferred communication biases, you will have gained all the information you need to help you begin guiding the direction of the conversation. Look for words and phrases such as:

- 武 I *see* what you mean.
- 武 I *hear* what you say.
- 武 I can *feel* it coming together.

- 武 I *smell* a rat.
- 武 I *understand* what you say.

Let's explore the fascinating concept of communication somatotyping. This unique system, which I developed, involves identifying word clues in phrases to categorise your opponent's communication biases. During a longer conversation, you can pick up several of these clues, enhancing your ability to understand your opponent's preferred communication style accurately.

Somatotyping and Communication

Communication somatotyping, a system I've devised, is a unique way of classifying human communication biases. It draws its roots from the field of human physiology, specifically the study of body types known as somatotyping. This process, which I'll explain in detail, is crucial to understanding how different individuals communicate.

In physical terms, the pure Endomorphic body is typically characterised by having a wide waist and larger bones, otherwise known as fat. The pure Mesomorphic body typically has wide shoulders, a narrow waist, a medium bone structure, and low body fat, otherwise known as muscular. The pure Ectomorphic body is typically characterised by having a slim chest, longer limbs, leaner muscles, and low fat, otherwise known as slim.

This classification system was developed in the 1940s by William Sheldon, a noted American psychologist. His system categorised the listed body types on a scale from 1 to 7. Using this scale, a pure Endomorphic body would be classified as being 7-1-1, with a pure Mesomorphic body being 1-7-1 and a pure Ectomorphic body being 1-1-7. Therefore, the somatotype of every person is expressed as three numbers in succession. For example, I would estimate that the somatotype of Arnold Schwarzenegger, arguably the greatest bodybuilder ever lived, would be approximately 2-6-2 on the Sheldon scale. Incidentally, I believe that

Arnold is also one of the World's great natural Mental Martial Artists. He has fantastic communication skills, uses his strong accent to his advantage, and was generally able to defeat many of his bodybuilding opponents psychologically before they even got onto the stage to compete against him. My reasons for giving Arnold the 2-6-2 somatotype are as follows:

- 武 He has a muscular face and square jaw.
- 武 Physically, he is almost the direct opposite of the Endomorph.
- 武 He has enormous muscular density.
- 武 He has the excellent biomechanical muscular insertions of a Mesomorph.
- 武 He has some of the characteristics of the Ectomorph with highly efficient lungs.

What's the link between physical somatotyping and communication? Just as a person's body can be classified into different types, so can their communication biases. We all have unique ways of thinking and reasoning, which shape how we send and receive communication. This means our communications are inherently biased towards our strongest preferences.

These biases can then be classified on a scale covering the five basic communication methods: visual, Auditory, Tactile, Olfactory, and Data. Using this method, a communication somatotype value can then be derived. The higher number represents a stronger bias, and the lower number represents a lesser bias.

The intention would be to use this communication system somatotyping to assess everyone you interact with rapidly. After a bit of practice, you should be able to rapidly assess the preferred communication biases of everyone you interact with. Once you have this information, you can use it to bias your communication with that person similarly. This will help them feel you understand and connect with them easily. It will also help you align your energy with them to help you direct the conversation's outcome.

To make learning the communication somatotyping system easier, remember the acronym I outlined earlier: V.A.T.O.D. It's a simple and memorable way to understand and apply all the communication biases. Rather than turning the pages back, I will recap it here:

- **V**isual
- **A**uditory
- **T**actile
- **O**lfactory
- **D**ata

This system works similarly to William Sheldon's physical somatotype scale. However, I have chosen to use a scale from 1 to 10 for the five communication categories.

The VATOD technique is surprisingly easy to use, and it can even become a source of great amusement when listening to certain people who very strongly fall into only one of the categories listed. Even though some people may have extreme leanings towards one bias, everyone will be classified as a combination of all five categories. Using this scale as follows:

- Someone with the strongest **V**isual bias possible and with all other biases at an absolute minimum would be classified as 10-1-1-1-1.
- Someone with the strongest **A**udible bias would be classified as being 1-10-1-1-1.
- Someone with the strongest **T**actile bias would be classified as being 1-1-10-1-1.
- Someone with the greatest **O**lfactory bias would be classified as being 1-1-1-10-1.
- Someone with the greatest **D**ata bias would be classified as being 1-1-1-1-10.

An example of a person with a neutral communication bias would probably be represented by the following combination: 6-5-4-3-5.

Developing Communication Somatotyping Skills

An excellent way of learning how to perform communication somatotyping is to start by treating it as a game. The ideal way to practice would be watching TV interviews and talk shows, especially if you can record the program to pause and then replay it. While you watch the TV news, journalists interview politicians, industrial leaders, celebrities, etc.

Make notes of the preferred communication characteristics of all parties in the conversation. Once you have scored each person's communication biases, see how fast you can learn to categorise the following people you observe. It will be fascinating if you spot any incongruence in the communication during an interview.

Once you have learned to categorise people quickly, you should be able to spot the preferred communication differences in real-time. If the differences between the communication biases of two people in a conversation are too great, it will quickly become apparent that although technically they may be speaking the same language, they completely fail to connect with and understand each other.

Communication somatotyping is not only a fun way to classify people according to their preferred biases; it is also an immensely powerful weapon for the mental martial artist. When you have shifted the ability to analyse people in this way into your subconscious mind, you will have greatly improved your overall communication and negotiation skills. You will then be able to begin incorporating other techniques, such as mirroring, to help you blend even more perfectly with your opponent.

Somatotype Word Bank

Here are some example words and phrases that are categorised according to their bias: visual, Audible, Tactile, Olfactory, or Data. This word bank will help you make more rapid decisions about which category words fall into during conversation. Your objective should be to subconsciously categorise words aromatically.

Visual Words

武	Colour	武	Notice
武	Dark	武	Look
武	Hazy	武	Picture
武	Horizon	武	Perspective
武	Scene	武	Insight
武	Visualise	武	Illusion
武	Shine	武	Foresight
武	Watch	武	Imagination
武	Clarify	武	Illustrate
武	Show	武	Reflect

Visual Phrases

武	Mind's eye	武	In X's blind spot
武	Seeing eye to eye	武	Hazy idea
武	Taking a dim view	武	No shadow of a doubt
武	Horizon	武	Shedding some light
武	I see what you mean	武	Show you what I mean

☐ Looking back	☐ Sight for sore eyes
☐ The future looks bright	☐ Looking through rose-tinted glasses

Auditory Words

☐ Echo	☐ Sounds
☐ Bell	☐ Click
☐ Resonate	☐ Buzz
☐ Crackle	☐ Sizzle
☐ Creak	☐ Shrill
☐ Mute	☐ Silence
☐ Deafening	☐ Vocal
☐ Whine	☐ Loudly

Auditory Phrases

☐ In harmony	☐ Living in harmony
☐ I hear what you say	☐ Same wavelength
☐ Manner of speaking	☐ That rings a bell
☐ Sell the sizzle	☐ Start with a bang
☐ Tumultuous reception	☐ Calls the tune

| ▪ Undertones to what was said | ▪ Dance to a different tune |

Tactile/Kinaesthetic Words

▪ Push	▪ Pull
▪ Gentle	▪ Firm
▪ Pressure	▪ Sensitive
▪ Sharp	▪ Blunt
▪ Sticky	▪ Slippery
▪ Solid	▪ Liquid
▪ Rough	▪ Smooth

Tactile/Kinaesthetic Phrases

▪ Getting in touch	▪ Scratch the surface
▪ Take control	▪ Firm hand
▪ Up and running	▪ Soft spot
▪ Breaking the mould	▪ Warm-hearted
▪ Hard case	▪ Surfing the net
▪ Falling to pieces	▪ Hold on a moment
▪ Heated discussion	▪ Tension in the air

Olfactory/Gustatory Words

☖ Nosey	☖ Stale
☖ Scented	☖ Smoky
☖ Smelly	☖ Sniff
☖ Fishy	☖ Fragrant

Olfactory/Gustatory Phrases

☖ Doesn't smell right	☖ Smell a rat
☖ Bitter experience	☖ Taste for adventure
☖ Fresh as a daisy	☖ Acidic words
☖ Smells fishy	☖ Sweet person
☖ Smell the roses	☖ Mouth-watering
☖ Smell the money	☖ Eat humble pie

Data Words

These words do not have any sensory connections and are neutral. This makes them an excellent choice when verbally blending with your opponent. They are wonderful words to draw your opponent into revealing their preferred communication biases while making you appear neutral.

☖ Data	☖ Evaluate
☖ Theorise	☖ Think
☖ Logic	☖ Model
☖ Attend	☖ Remember

武 Learn	武 Idea
武 Outcome	武 Result
武 Past	武 Present

Multiple Intelligences in Communication

Communication somatotyping has a natural connection with the concept of multiple intelligences. Howard Gardner first proposed the theory of multiple intelligences in 1983 as a way of differentiating intelligence into specific categories. His concept argued that learning was always linked to the individual's personal bias towards one of the categories outlined in the concept of multiple intelligences. It also suggested that just because someone has difficulty learning something in a certain way, it does not make them less intelligent than someone who can learn quickly.

Instead, what is required is to change the method or bias of the preferred way of receiving information. This would then enable them to learn more efficiently. Therefore, the concept of multiple intelligences should be factored into my idea of communication somatotyping. This will help you fine-tune your communication and your power of persuasion over others.

Logical and Data Biased Intelligence

Logical and data-biased intelligence is natural for left-brain thinkers comfortable with reasoning and logical critical thinking.

Spatial and Visualised Intelligence

Spatial and visualised intelligence falls into the category of the right-brained thinker who is comfortable with their mind-eye visualisation processes.

Linguistic Intelligence

People with linguistic intelligence learn best through words. Naturally, their preferred learning communication biases are through the mediums of writing, reading, speaking, or listening. Such people are usually eloquent and possess an excellent command of vocabulary and syntax.

Kinaesthetic and Bodily Intelligence

Those who are biased towards kinaesthetic and bodily intelligence are usually natural athletes who possess excellent control of their bodies. These people learn and communicate best via touch, manipulation, physical examination, and experimentation. They have a strong sense of natural timing and respond well to reflex training.

Auditory and Musical Intelligence

People with auditory and musical intelligence naturally respond best to sounds, music, tone, and rhythm. Such people are often exceptionally skilled in multiple languages and respond well to seminar-style presentations and communication.

Interpersonal Intelligence

People who are biased towards possessing interpersonal intelligence for both learning and communication usually respond best when interacting with others. They are generally good team players, thrive when working in groups, and are typically good at sensing the moods and feelings of others.

Intrapersonal Intelligence

Those who possess what is called intrapersonal intelligence usually have empathy toward others. They typically understand the needs and feelings of others, and they also tend to enjoy discussion and debate. Such individuals are also able to reflect and introspect easily and are often seen to have a deep understanding of their strengths and weaknesses. They are usually gifted at predicting their reactions and emotional responses to external happenings.

Naturalistic Intelligence

Those classified as biased towards naturalistic intelligence are strongly connected to the earth and the environment. They are usually very much in tune with nature and easily connect with others when relating to such associations.

Existential Intelligence

Individuals biased towards the controversial existential intelligence classification might be said to possess spiritual intelligence. Howard Gardner did not include this classification in his original work, possibly because he did not want to commit to believing in spiritual intelligence in front of his peers.

Those said to possess this intelligence bias would learn and communicate best with phenomena beyond the range of standard sensory data. A genius such as the great Stephen Hawking might be said to possess such intelligence due to his ability to conceptualise theoretical physics.

Voice Production

Your voice is vital to effective communication. The power and effect created by a great orator such as Sir Winston Churchill are almost incalculable. Therefore, to master every aspect of Mental Martial Arts, you should also learn how to master your voice.

The objective is to master the tone, pitch, rhythm, intonation, volume, and what I call the flavour of your voice. As with many things in life, it is comparatively easy to objectively advise others on what might be best for them.

However, it is often difficult to be objective about ourselves. The same is true with speech. It is typically easy to tell others what is wrong with their voice, while at the same time, we cannot always spot our flaws.

This is partly because we listen to our voice through the dense bone structure of our skull. Therefore, we cannot hear ourselves quite like other people do. This is also why some people are shocked when they listen to their voices played back from a recording device for the first time. Since your face did not come with a pause, record, or playback button, it is worth practising vocal exercises with a voice recorder. The main terms used for defining vocal qualities are:

Volume

Volume is how loud your voice sounds. You should be able to easily adjust the volume of your voice according to your surroundings while still being heard clearly without shouting.

Pitch

Pitch is how low or high your voice is. You should aim to slightly lower your pitch. This technique tends to draw the listener towards you. You can also use it to emphasise an important point or to distract from a weak point.

Rhythm

Rhythm is the beat of your voice, and you should always try to avoid speaking too quickly. Talking too fast will cause words to clash, making them a verbal barrage to the listener.

It can also cause the syllables to become clipped and shortened, which creates confusion and the impression that you are nervous. By talking a little slower, your words will naturally lengthen, and varying your rhythm helps to maintain the interest of your audience.

Tone

The tone is the perceived characteristic of your voice. We all know the different characteristics and tones of an angry voice as opposed to the voice of a happy person. Study your tone and composition of tonal characteristics. This will enable you to alter the tone of your voice more efficiently according to your objectives.

Intonation

Intonation is the way you combine pitch, tone, and rhythm. If used correctly, proper intonation will greatly increase your power of persuasion. Study the intonation of some of the great movie actors; this way, you will probably learn something useful while you are being entertained!

Droll

A droll is a speaking style typically used by hypnotists to induce a trance in a listener. This technique is also used by many in the legal profession because it helps them to emphasise a point during public litigation.

When speaking with a droll, your voice will be paced as if timed by a metronome, placing particular emphasis on each word. Delivering your droll at around 50 to 55 words per minute will help induce a state of suggestion in those listening. It is also good to practice combining your pace, tone, speed, and volume to ensure a well-rounded and robust message delivery.

Flavour

Flavour is the character of "you" in your conversation. We are all different, so we all have different characters. Some prefer to blend into the background, while others enjoy the limelight. No matter what, you will naturally be a great character in your unique way. Be proud of this and develop it by adding your distinctive flavour. It will serve to enhance the power of "you."

Enunciation, Elongated Vowels and Concrete Consonants

Using elongated vowels and concrete consonants is a simple and highly effective way to help improve both your Received Pronunciation and your General Enunciation. Received Pronunciation is regarded as the standard accent of Standard English. The elongated vowel is usually associated with 'baby-speak' or 'pet-speak.'

This is when everyday speech changes to enable the voice to be heard more clearly. We have all done this in one form or another when encountering a friend's new baby, kitten, or puppy. It is almost automatic that we immediately change how we speak in everyday conversation and begin speaking more slowly, emphasising elongated vowels and consonants.

The slightly elongated vowels and emphasised consonants will also slightly reduce your regular speed of speech delivery. This is a good thing since most people usually speak far too fast, especially when speaking in public or appearing on video.

The bonus factor is that this technique will give you far better diction and enunciation. When practised and mastered, these techniques will make you appear more polished and experienced as a presenter on stage or on camera.

Improve Your Voice and Delivery

Practice listening to your voice and its various component characteristics by reading passages aloud from books, magazines, or newspapers. Make a recording as you do so, and during the replay, always be objective and open to improvement.

There is usually a voice recorder on your cell phone; however, if you do not have one, try using your hand as a hearing aid. You do this by cupping one hand around your ear and carefully pulling it forward; you then cup your other hand next to your mouth. Using your hands in this way enables you to channel the sound in the direction of your ear so you can hear yourself as others listen to you.

- 武 Monitor your voice during general everyday conversation. Check that you are using words properly and delivering them with your desired phrasing, rhythm, tone, intonation, etc.
- 武 Learn to mirror your vocal tone, rhythm, and intonation with those you communicate with. The voice mirroring action, combined with incorporating physical mirroring gestures, will have an amazing effect on your control of the conversation. You will usually find that those you communicate with will be much more relaxed with you and that the conversation will generally flow more easily.
- 武 Develop your unique vocal characteristics and skills as a budding orator. Always practice speaking as if you are presenting on stage.
- 武 Learn to project your voice without appearing to shout. Projection is the delivery of your voice to the desired point, usually some distance away. This involves the combined use of volume, pitch, tone, intonation, and diaphragm control. Stage actors learn this technique to be able to deliver their dialogue clearly to the rear of the theatre.
- 武 Check your overall presentation style by standing in front of a mirror, preferably a full-length one, while you read the various passages aloud. This will allow you to evaluate your whole physical presence exactly as your opponent would see you.

Syntax and Emphasis

Syntax is the emphasis placed upon a word in a sentence or phrase. For example, take the simple sentence: "I didn't say we trained together." First, please say this phrase aloud without emphasising any word in the sentence. Next, please repeat the same sentence aloud while placing the most significant emphasis on the word in bold in the following:

- "**I** didn't say we trained together".
- "I **didn't** say we trained together".
- "I didn't **say** we trained together".
- "I didn't say **we** trained together".
- "I didn't say we **trained** together".
- "I didn't say we trained **together**".

Having completed this exercise, you will now more fully understand the enormous power of using something as simple as the correct syntax. As always, it is not just what you say that counts; it is also how you say it.

Friendly Persuasion and Boiling Frogs

We all use persuasion every day, and it is an art we first learned as children. Persuasion is the ability to influence or change the beliefs, motivations, attitudes, or intentions of others. In an earlier section, I compared the different characteristics of left and right-brain thinkers. I outlined how the left brain is rational and analytical, while the right brain is creative and emotional. These factors can be of enormous assistance in learning the art of persuasion. The objective is to distract your opponent's left brain, which is the analytical and logical side, while you engage your opponent's right brain, which is the emotional and creative side. This simple technique dramatically increases your overall power of persuasion. As you will see shortly, this is the same technique politicians have been taught to master to help influence voters.

The technique I call boiling a frog is also about persuasion, and I am not implying or suggesting that anyone should ever actually boil a real frog. What does it mean then? In theory, if you brought a pan of water to a boil and then tossed a frog into it, the chances are that it would immediately jump straight out. After a few attempts, and with an increasingly scalded frog, you may get it to stay in the water and be boiled. However, there is a much easier way to do this. The best way to boil a frog is to persuade it to be boiled willingly. How do you achieve this? You do this by getting the frog to agree with you and metaphorically say "yes" to being boiled. Place a pan of room-temperature water on the stove, then drop your frog in. Since the water will initially be at room temperature, the frog will likely stay in the pan and happily swim around. You then switch on the stove. The water begins to heat up very gradually, and as it does so, the frog enjoys the increasingly warming water. Using this process, your frog is relaxing, not even realising it is being boiled. The frog can only feel the warm water, which makes it increasingly tired until it eventually drifts to sleep, and its fate is sealed.

How do you persuade people to be metaphorically 'boiled?' You use the same strategy and get them to say "yes" to the idea of being boiled. The difference is that you are not boiling a person. Instead, you are persuading someone to agree with your point of view. To do this, you use the power of agreement combined with your knowledge of how each of the two halves of the human brain functions. You distract your opponent's left brain, which is the logical side, while at the same time engaging, appealing to, and persuading their right brain, which is the emotional side.

You begin the process by engaging your opponent's left brain by getting them to agree to a series of logical statements and facts repeatedly. Perhaps you could throw a little confusion into the mix by adding an element of obscure knowledge that will more fully engage their left brain. Your objective is to get your opponent to agree with you by saying the word "yes." This simple act of agreement can be a powerful tool in your persuasion arsenal.

To help you achieve your objective more quickly, you may wish to add a physical gesture while you speak, such as a nod of the head at an appropriate moment, which will then support the suggestion that they agree with you. Your opponent will probably subconsciously pick up this movement, and eventually, they will begin to mirror your head nod. This physical reinforcement on their part will increase their emotional and intellectual agreement with you.

Once you have got your opponent agreeing with you about hard facts, you begin to shift emphasis. Slowly and carefully shift from the agreement of facts to whatever it is that you want to persuade them to do, think, or believe. Since you have already begun reinforcing your verbal messages with physical agreements, it is less likely that your opponent will notice and consciously decline your suggestion. If you do all of this subtly enough from the start, then they will probably continue to agree with you. This process requires finesse and skill, but when executed well, it can be highly effective.

An excellent way to observe this technique is when a politician seeks re-election. Politicians will engage their listeners' logical left brain with facts and figures about the economy, crime, etc. They may even support this by comparing facts, examining figures, and data from other countries. This process engages the left brain with hard data. Furthermore, it is doubtful that the data they use will be already known to the listener. Therefore, it cannot easily be refuted, denied, or contradicted. Next, the politician will engage the listener's emotional right side of the brain, which is the creative side. They will create images with words intended to stir the listener's base emotions and feelings about things like poverty, hunger, crime, and fear. Their speech might go something like this.

"Are you upset at the increasingly high food prices in your stores?"

This delivery will be accompanied by a slight head nod from the politician to suggest agreement.

"Are you sick and tired of increasing unemployment?"

Again, this will be accompanied by a slight head nod from the politician to suggest agreement. Next, they will begin to make their vocal presentation a little more dramatic.

"Are you tired of spending every penny that you earn on fuel for your cars and to heat your homes?"

Once again, this delivery will be accompanied by a slight head nod from the politician to suggest agreement. Their vocal presentation will now become a little slower to emphasise what is being said, and they will emphasise the word 'you' to add weight to the message's delivery.

"Are you scared to walk the streets at night because the police are failing to protect you, the innocent taxpayer?"

This delivery will once again be accompanied by a slight head nod from the politician to suggest agreement. Now, the right brain of the audience has been engaged, and their emotions are being fully charged. The politician will then deliver some baffling statistics about inflation, fuel prices, crime, etc., and in doing so, they will completely engage the listener's left brain. Finally, the politician will suggest what they want in the following way:

"We need to solve these problems quickly. We need decisive action, not just more words. The answer to solving these problems and others like them is to re-elect me to parliament."

The politician will also have been using strategic syntax to help create strategic emphasis and reinforce what they are saying. Almost all successful politicians are highly trained in this technique, and experts in the art of suggestion write their speeches.

Another example of a persuasive suggestion which might be in a TV news report could be something like this:

"Councillor Harris has put a motion forward aimed at helping the police to tackle crime."

To most listeners, this will sound like a typical news statement of fact. However, it is not. Emphasising the keywords 'helping' and 'tackling' makes it a persuasive suggestion. It makes it seem that the report is saying that Councillor Harris is helping the police tackle crime. Of course, this is not what has been said.

In various parts of the world, television and print news media are sometimes jointly owned by individuals with a particular political agenda. This renders the so-called news reports made by those networks little more than political persuasion and even pure nonsense. In some cases, specific news channels would be more honest if they began their news reports with the words: "Once upon a time..." and ended the report with the words: "They all lived happily ever after." The reality is that often, what they have reported as 'fact' is little more than a fairytale. During my time with BBC TV News, we frequently reported the same stories as TV news crews from across the Atlantic. However, the content of each report was often quite different, with ours being comparatively neutral in delivery and without persuasion.

Unfortunately, the BBC has become riddled with all kinds of bias, so it is far less neutral in the information it disseminates than when I worked there. The real moral of the story here is never to underestimate the power of persuasion, and beware because it can come disguised in many forms and from all directions.

Questions, Questions, Questions

The overall quality of your questions is not just important; it's crucial. When you ask better, quality questions, you receive more high-quality data back as a result. Therefore, you are not just a passive recipient but an active participant in the communication process. You are technically only as good as the quality of the questions you ask because the data you receive will affect the decisions you make.

Always express yourself clearly and politely to get the answers you want. Quality questions combined with good listening techniques will help to maximise the quality of data you receive. As you ask a question, you should also use mirroring and blending techniques to make your opponent feel at ease. Make your questions succinct and relevant to the conversation. They should be well-composed and comprised of strategically balanced content. The questions you ask may also contain positive or negative biases, which can, in turn, help to influence the outcome of the conversation significantly. This underscores the power you hold in shaping conversations through the questions you ask.

A positively biased question that will usually get agreement from your listener might be phrased as follows:

"I'm sure you'd enjoy a deliciously cool ice cream?"

Naturally, it would be delivered with the correct emphasis, syntax, tone, etc., to deliver the desired positive bias. This is a very positive statement that is made to appear to be a question. The same question could equally be asked with a negative bias, which would typically achieve a negative response. This might be phrased as follows:

"You wouldn't like some ice cream, would you?"

Biasing your questions in this way will usually lead your opponent into the belief pattern of your choice, often without them realising. Therefore, if you want to exert a primary influence, you should always bias your questions according to the desired outcome. An excellent way of practising this technique is simply engaging a friend in general social conversation. Use words and phrases such as:

- 武 I am sure you agree.
- 武 As we know.
- 武 As we agreed earlier.
- 武 As we know for sure.
- 武 Just as you pointed out.
- 武 Just as you mentioned.

Remember, effective communication is not just about the words you use. It's about the correct emphasis, syntax, tone, and even your body language. These elements, when used in harmony, can significantly enhance your delivery. Once you've established common ground, you can then apply other Mental Martial Arts techniques to steer the conversation's direction. This approach has the added advantage of making your opponent feel they've contributed to the agreed-upon points, fostering a more positive relationship.

This kind of communication bias is easy to use, and if needed, it can be an enormously powerful conversation-closing tool. However, as with all martial arts, timing is critical. Always maintain your guard, and never underestimate any opponent. It is also worth considering that it might be you who is being guided in conversation by someone who is even more skilled at Mental Martial Arts than you are. In such circumstances, your opponent may wish you to believe they are less competent than you to catch you off guard. Always be aware of the unassuming characters who seem to pass almost unnoticed. Experience has taught me that some of these people can be the most dangerous opponents you will ever encounter.

Combat Questions

The art of asking and replying to questions can be linked to how you engage an opponent in physical combat. Metaphorically, similar techniques are used to probe an opponent for potential weaknesses and to test their strengths. In Mental Martial Arts, you would probe your opponent by initially asking lighter, less direct questions. Using this technique in the early stages of verbal engagement is helpful, and your opponent probably will not feel as though they are under immediate attack.

Direct, well-timed, targeted, and well-composed questions containing the correct biases will usually get good results. Using this technique, you can probe your opponent's vital knowledge and the real meaning behind their words. Once you have mastered these techniques, you can begin reading your opponent before leading your opponent.

If you have detailed prior knowledge of the meeting, starting the engagement with some direct questions is a good idea. However, the reality of any combat situation is that the first casualty in the engagement is usually the plan. So be prepared for this in advance, and do not be surprised if your well-rehearsed plan suddenly falls apart. If this happens, you must either improvise, adapt, and overcome the problem or become metaphorically 'dead in the water.'

Once fully engaged, your opponent must have no idea that they have caught you off guard and that you are suddenly improvising. As far as your opponent is concerned, nothing should alert them to any problems you might have. Naturally, this requires rapid realisation, improvisation, and implementing a new strategy, all without showing a sign that anything is wrong.

Probing combat questions can also clarify important points during a conversation. This can be especially useful if you need additional thinking time. Do not let an unanswered question by your opponent disturb you. Furthermore, do not be unnerved by questions returned to you by your opponent in the form of another question or by questions deliberately intended to throw you off on a tangent. If your opponent uses this technique, it might suggest that they are unsettled or being guarded as they try to hide something.

Your response should be like a rounded or hooked movement in physical combat. Begin by envisioning yourself assuming a circular or spherical form. This shape can quickly move, flow, and redirect energy. In doing so, you might also envision how such a metaphysical form might deflect and re-channel the energy of a hooked attack by your opponent and then re-channel it back in a circular motion.

You should then attempt to redirect your opponent's energy by pausing, probing, and clarifying specific points about what your opponent has just said. Using that information allows you to re-group your thoughts before returning the question with another similar 'hooked' question. By rephrasing and re-biasing an immediate response aimed at the same target, you will essentially return it in a circular motion from which they may not easily recover.

The Caesura

Never underestimate the value of a well-timed caesura or pause. A simple pause can buy valuable thinking time, help you appear to be listening more intently, or destabilise your opponent and set them off balance. The insertion of an unnatural caesura in what would be a natural conversation flow is a real attention grabber. This technique will force your opponent to pay more attention to what you are saying and leave them more vulnerable to your probing questions. Watching a skilled master of the unnatural pause in action, then just watching the great movie actor John Wayne. John Wayne, a personal favourite, fully understood the power of persuasion with words. He was a far more highly skilled actor than most people ever realised.

More importantly, he knew exactly where and when to place the unnatural caesura to break the dialogue and then gain greater emphasis. He developed this technique when working with the classic movie director John Ford, so you can find many excellent examples of this technique in the movies they made together.

Repeat - Repeat

Another technique I highly recommend you practice is repeating. I mean that you repeat aloud the essential points of your opponent's questions or conversation as part of your reply. This technique not only buys you valuable additional thinking time but also ensures that you properly engage the main points of your opponent's conversation.

If your opponent is not completely satisfied with how you have answered their question, it is highly likely that the question will linger on and could become a bigger problem for you later. If you are not careful, you might even have the balance of the engagement turned on you, with your opponent doing the leading and with you scrambling to recover.

During the conversation, try to maintain empathy with your opponent; however, do not ever allow yourself to develop sympathy. There is nothing wrong with understanding how someone feels; however, being drawn into feeling the same way as someone else is generally not a particularly good idea. There is a world of difference between the two terminologies, and they are often easily confused.

Be Direct

A well-targeted or direct approach is usually best, either in response to others' questioning or when you are the person asking the questions. Remember to use interesting anecdotes and stories, which will always add flavour and richness to your presentation. These will help you engage your listeners more fully and substantially reinforce what you are communicating. However, do not let the anecdote or story detract from the overall impact of your direct questions and statements.

When I worked with BBC TV News, it was common knowledge that viewers always tended to remember the high-impact first line of the news reports. In the same way, viewers and listeners will also usually remember the last line of your statement, question, or presentation. These techniques are known as a 'strong opening' or a 'strong close.' Both techniques work equally well in general conversations, meetings, negotiations, and presentations. The first and last line rule is an immensely powerful weapon that you can deploy when you need it. The Shaolin teach:

"Always beware the sheep, for who is to say that it is not a wolf in disguise?"

The Art of Listening

Listening is just as much part of good communication as talking. However, many people are exceedingly poor listeners. I am sure you will recall your mother or father telling you that you do not learn anything by talking and only learn things by listening. They were right. When trying to get a point across or win an argument, some people simply launch an uncoordinated verbal assault. Such people will rapid-fire their words almost without taking a breath. When dealing with people like this, no matter what the receiver says in response or how loudly they say it, they are not being heard.

Listening is an art that requires a little practice to become good at. There are many benefits of being a good listener for the Mental Martial Artist because it is the perfect way to gain the vital intelligence you need about an opponent. The best part is that your opponent will be naturally encouraged to talk because most people love to talk about themselves.

It is pretty easy to hear what someone is saying; however, that is superficial compared to power listening. Power Listening requires deep concentration and a proper real-time evaluation of what is being said to assess the information strategically. The basics of good Power Listening are as follows:

- 武 Do not complete another person's sentences.
- 武 Do not make assumptions.
- 武 Do not let your ego take over and allow you to dominate the conversation.
- 武 Do not answer questions with other questions unless it is intentional.
- 武 Do not let your mind wander; always concentrate fully on what is being said.
- 武 Do not interrupt.
- 武 Formulate careful, strategic responses while still listening carefully.
- 武 Occasionally, confirm and agree with what is being said by paraphrasing the person who is talking.

If necessary, and with the correct timing, you should ask pertinent questions during the conversation. This will help to avoid any possible misunderstandings which may arise. Having a wandering mind that inadvertently drifts into daydreaming or onto other subjects is the enemy of power listening. During any conversation, your complete concentration is required. It is that simple. Learning the art of Power Listening and how to use it instinctively can completely transform your conversations. You will shift from being constantly confused to one of greater communication, understanding, and balance.

Silence is Golden

Silence may be likened to being golden; however, silence is also an immensely powerful weapon. When used correctly, silence can encourage your opponent to become drawn into saying or agreeing with something they would not necessarily wish to in other circumstances.

Why does silence have this effect? It's a psychological response because the mind dislikes even verbal vacuums. Have you ever noticed how some people use filler words during TV interviews or public speaking? These are words like:

- "Err".
- "Right".
- "You know".
- "As I said earlier".
- "So".

Silence leaves a gap or a mental vacuum. During a conversation, the human brain almost compels us to fill that vacuum with something rather than just leaving it blank and pausing for a second. This anomaly in how we are all mentally wired can be used as an effective weapon by the Mental Martial Artist.

With the correct strategic use in a conversation, adding a deliberate and well-timed silence can lead your opponent to agree to what is being said to fill the vacuum you have created.

The G-8 Technique

The G-8 technique is a potent public speaking tip I learned several years ago when attending the 1998 G-8 global summit in Birmingham, England, for BBC TV news. The G-8 summit was the annual meeting of the heads of state from the world's eight leading industrial nations. Naturally, such an event is incredibly demanding for all concerned, and an opportunity to take even a five-minute break is always more than welcome. There was a time when the TV crew I was leading encountered technical issues with a satellite feed that was beyond our control, so we were blessed with a short break.

We were then our interview subject, Mr Jacques Santier, who welcomed the short unscheduled break, which gave him time to enjoy a coffee until our technical issues were fixed. At that time, Jacques Santier was the president of the European Union and was generally regarded as one of Europe's great orators.

During the break, we chatted and shared ideas about public speaking. Among the many stories and broadcasting techniques we shared, one immediately caught my attention. Mr Santier told me that he had learned a particularly effective technique that allowed him to seamlessly fill in gaps during interviews, conversations, and even formal presentations.

More importantly, this technique usually left audiences blissfully unaware that he had even paused for thought. He explained how he found this technique especially valuable when under extreme pressure during a tough TV interview or when he was in a debate and under pressure to answer a difficult or complex question that needed some extra thinking time. He called the technique his 'Semi-Coherent Mode.'

The technique he used was to carry on speaking when he found himself in trouble. Instead of using the more usual filler words that inexperienced people would, he used generic words and phrases that were related in some way to the subject matter. He explained that so long as the words and phrases were related in some way to the subject matter or the broad philosophies surrounding it, then whatever he said would seem to make some sense. In other words, he would be talking a lot yet saying little. He was effectively using a more sophisticated set of filler words and phrases. Mr Santier told me that he would continue to use this technique until he had picked up the thread of his conversation and could respond to the thorny question appropriately.

I called what Mr Santier called his 'Semi-Coherent Mode:' Conversation Flow. Conversation Flow is a simple and amazingly effective technique. Once you have mastered it, you will never be stuck during a conversation again, and you will certainly never need to resort to using the more common ugly filler words. Whatever you say will generally sound coherent, professional, and polished; with only a little practice, making the simple mental notes required during a conversation that can be used, if needed, as a Conversation Flow filler is not hard.

Remember, what you say as a conversation filler does not matter too much; the important thing is that it should always be connected to your subject matter in some way. This technique may feel odd initially because you will know that the words and phrases you use do not contain any actual content. However, the audience is generally a few steps behind you and typically will not even notice.

I asked Mr Santier if he had devised this technique, but he had not. Instead, I was astonished to learn that it was a technique taught to him by Baroness Margaret Thatcher, the former Prime Minister of Great Britain. This should not be surprising because she was among the most outstanding and powerful public speakers ever. Naturally, it is not a new technique because since politics first began, all politicians have usually talked a lot while saying little of any real value. The next time you see a politician being interviewed on television, watch out for their Conversation Flow moments and judge how good they are at using the technique.

When you next find yourself under the spotlight and stuck for words, it is too late to do anything except mumble embarrassingly or dry up completely. Practice this technique in advance because conversation flow works well and can save you from public embarrassment.

Ki-ai

The Ki-ai, pronounced Key-eye, is an interesting footnote to verbal communications. Some of the harder, external forms of martial arts use the power of the voice to enhance their physical power. This is known as Ki-ai. Ki-ai is the sound made by the practitioners of Karate when delivering a powerful blow in combat or when breaking blocks.

The sound is made as the air is forcefully expelled from the body and as the martial artist's Chi energy emanates from their core to focus on the target. This simple technique helps martial artists greatly increase their physical power. I also know that it works because I have used it many times, particularly when I performed both of my successful block-breaking world records.

> *"Do not despise the snake for having no horns, for who is to say that one day it will not become a dragon?"*

In short, do not mock what you do not yet understand.

Non-Verbal Communication - Shapeshifting

A physical martial artist often uses mirroring techniques to assume positions and stances similar to their opponent's. This is because mirroring usually affords them a better offensive or defensive position. However, mirroring will also have the effect of subtly making their opponent feel slightly more at ease. In turn, this can sometimes cause them to relax their guard slightly. What is mirroring? Mirroring is a behaviour where we copy someone else during an interaction with them. Mirroring includes assuming similar:

- Stances
- Postures
- Voice inflexion and tone
- Eye movements
- Hand positions and general gestures
- Breathing rates
- Word and phrase choices
- General attitude

When people are engaged in general conversation with a friend, they often naturally mirror each other without even realising it. This is because it is a technique we have all learned from an early age. In body language terms, mirroring is a way to subconsciously bond with and build trust with whoever you are in conversation with. For example, take a simple smile. Even if you are not feeling especially happy, seeing someone smile generally makes you want to smile, too. Yawning is the same. If you see someone yawn, then you are almost certainly going to yawn yourself within a minute of seeing it.

Scientists have discovered that there is a neuron in our brain which is responsible for us being able to recognise faces and expressions. Furthermore, this neuron is responsible for our use of mirroring. The body language expression of mirroring sends the message that 'we are the same' and 'I am like you.' Scientists have also discovered that people who feel similar emotions build greater trust and connection. In social groups, people tend to mirror and feel the same emotions. They will also begin to match their body language and other expressions subconsciously. Interestingly, scientists have discovered that the human brain has regions that sympathetically respond to pain and pleasure in others.

You can usually observe mirroring techniques used effectively during TV interviews, making this an excellent way of learning the art for yourself. Look for the subtle imitation of gestures that send non-verbal signals that they better understand each other's opinions and perspectives.

You should also be aware of people mirroring you, especially if someone mirrors you too quickly and perfectly. Those who do this are probably deliberately mirroring to win your trust; they may even attempt to form some relationship with you. If someone is naturally mirroring you, you will almost certainly be unaware that this is happening because it will be subtle. Therefore, before you use mirroring as a technique, it is worth practising first to become proficient at deliberately mirroring without other people realising what you are doing. If you must move slightly to better mirror your opponent, do not move too soon. Instead, wait between 10 and 15 seconds before assuming your new, mirrored response to your opponent and always do it slowly, naturally, and subtly.

Interestingly, when I studied video recordings of interviews between a potential new employee and an employer, it reinforced the power of the mirroring technique. When I compared the video footage and support information about who was short-listed for the job and why, some interesting yet unsurprising results emerged. The interviewer's notes clearly showed that the candidates who used the mirroring technique were always better thought of. Indeed, the winning candidate used the mirroring technique during the interview process. I am not sure if they were deliberately using the technique or not because it certainly seemed to be natural.

I once interviewed Professor Chris Dede for a TV news article and was fascinated to learn about a research study about morphing. This was of interest to me because I considered the method and results to be somewhat reminiscent of advanced mirroring. Chris Dede is a fascinating character, and interviewing him is always a great pleasure. He is the Timothy E. Worth Learning Professor at Harvard University in the U.S.A. Furthermore, Chris is generally acknowledged as one of the world's leading authorities on learning and education. One of his areas of expertise is emerging technologies in education.

During the interview, he told me about the research performed by Jeremy Bailenson, an expert in Transformed Social Interaction, or TSI, at Stanford School of Communications. This research was conducted on social interaction and engagement for educators.

In the virtual world, educators can now appear to interact with student viewers on a one-to-one basis. As part of this work, Jeremy Bailenson uncovered some extremely interesting findings concerning how people feel most comfortable and at ease during their interactions with others. In the experiment, he used morphing technology in tests conducted on participants during the 2008 U.S. elections.

In doing so, he semi-morphed his participants' faces into the election candidates' faces; in this case, it was that of George Bush. However, he did not completely morph one into the other. He stopped short at the 60-40 level of morph, a point just below the human level of conscious recognition of change. At this level, the participants in the study would think they were still watching and interacting with a virtual George Bush. However, the version of George Bush they were interacting with had been subtly morphed to look a little like each participant in the study. The experiment results showed that people felt a much stronger affinity to the 60-40 slightly morphed image they interacted with than the non-morphed image.

Morphing can be directly likened to a very advanced form of mirroring. I also believe that these findings are extremely significant and that more research will clearly show the persuasive power of what I call Perception Morphing. By using all possible mirroring factors, including verbal, intellectual, physical, emotional, etc., it is possible to create a high degree of Perception Morphing with others at a subconscious level.

This will make those you interact with feel similar to you, as the test subjects felt towards the images morphed in the experiment. The Perception Morphing technique is perhaps the closest way possible for real-life human interactions to achieve similar results to those gained in the experiments conducted by Jeremy Bailenson.

Take the most famous quote of the English writer Charles Caleb *Colton*:

"Imitation is the sincerest form of flattery."

If that is the case, then mirroring is precisely that. Undoubtedly, it is a potent technique for helping build a good relationship and rapport with your opponent. Try it for yourself the next time you want to subtly win your spouse over to your point of view!

Body Language

It is a fact that everyone on the planet who is physically interacting with another person will also continuously send and receive nonverbal signals and messages. These nonverbal signals communicate many things, such as happiness, sadness, relaxation, anger, interest, or complete disinterest. Collectively, these nonverbal communication messages are known as body language.

You are probably aware that it was Albert Mehrabian who, as a Professor of Psychology at UCLA, studied all forms of communication and, in doing so, made some startling findings. His original published findings became famously known as the '7%-38%-55%' rule. This showed in terms of percentages how our communication is weighted, received, and understood by others. Surprisingly, Professor Mehrabian found that words make up only 7% of our communication bias, tone makes up 38%, and perhaps most startlingly, an astonishing 55% of our communication comes from non-verbal signals. However, I believe the reality is probably more of a constantly sliding scale around the original percentile index points for each.

Body language is an integral part of human communication. As such, we are usually unaware of the myriad of subtle macro signals we all make during conversations with others. Body language is so ingrained in us that even when we speak to someone by phone and they can't see us, we still express the same body language messages as if they were right in front of us. We use these body language messages to reinforce our verbal communications. The subtle body language movements comprise what is known technically as paralanguage. This is a term that covers all forms of basic non-verbal human communication. These subtle macro signals include facial expressions, scratching the head or arms, rubbing the nose, and various eye movements, including blinking. You will become aware of many others as you think about and study the concept.

Taking body language as part of a greater whole within our communication arsenal, there are many other factors to be considered when attempting to interpret the real meaning of other people. There are often many different reasons why people express specific characteristics with their body language, many of which may have little or no connection to their feelings. Undoubtedly, Professor Mehrabian's research results have been highly significant in improving our understanding of communication. However, I believe that too much significance may have been placed on a narrowly focused area of communication at the expense of the greater whole. Indeed, some people have even built complete strategies surrounding those findings alone.

In attempting to control your body language, sending mixed and confusing messages is relatively easy. Thanks to our body language, it is not easy to lie because there are around 90 muscles in the human face and over 600 muscles in the body. Tests have proven that even the highest level of professional poker players all express minute signals, which can give away the strength of their hand to an opponent. Studies have shown that when a player receives a poor hand, they tend to look at the cards slightly longer than they would if their hand were good. Similarly, if their hand is good, their blink rate increases slightly. A highly skilled poker player who is also highly experienced in body language might use body language, or reverse body language, to dupe an opponent. Therefore, many other factors must be carefully considered and factored into interpreting the overall equation to accurately 'read' a situation.

Learning to control the many muscles needed to lie convincingly through your expressed body language is challenging. Actors train for years to learn and master such techniques, which is also why method acting is so effective. It is easier for an actor to completely immerse themselves in the role to project a complete image of the character they are portraying. I believe that body language can be effectively and deliberately used to support other forms of communication. It is also particularly good at helping you to assess your deepest feelings. Your subconscious mind will tell you, via your body language, precisely what you feel at any given moment.

Examples of Body Language and Possible Meanings

If a person crosses their arms, then it may be perceived to be a classic barrier signal or a way in which we non-verbally distance or protect ourselves from something. However, it should also be considered that the person crossing their arms may not be putting up a barrier signal at all. They may be more comfortable in that position for various physical reasons, such as having a muscle strain or injury or perhaps because they are cold. It is essential to look for additional sub-signals to interpret a person's real meaning more accurately from their body language. These signals often contain valuable information, such as arm or hand rubbing to warm up or perhaps touching, massaging, or favouring a joint, muscle or limb that might be injured.

Despite the many possible variations in interpreting the real meaning behind the crossing of the arms gesture, it is still widely accepted as a potent subconscious barrier signal to onlookers. In a potential confrontation situation, the arms-crossed action may indicate that your opponent is expressing serious opposition to you. The additional sub-factors of their leaning away from you or their facial expressions may combine to support this. If a speaker or a corporate representative uses the arms crossed gesture as they speak, their audience is less receptive to receiving the message they wish to convey. It distances both them and their message from their audience. It may even suggest that the presenter is not connected with the feelings or emotions of the audience. Therefore, you should know what signals you wish to convey, primarily through innocent or inadvertent gestures.

Talking without using your hands would not feel right, especially if you are right-brain dominant. To observe this in action, watch the TV news and pay attention to the body language of the news correspondents compared to those being interviewed. It will be an interesting exercise, especially when a politician is being 'grilled' by a skilled journalist over a problematic point. It is also a good idea to note the vocal and facial expressions used and the hand actions of TV news broadcasters. Also, please carefully note their voice's pace, tone, and intonation as they convey either good or bad news.

Eye to Eye

Eye contact is one of the most significant forms of non-verbal communication. Furthermore, where and how a person looks can convey valuable information about how they think and prefer to receive communications. If you are conversing with someone and they look upwards while thinking, their bias is visual. If they look downward, their bias is tactile, and if they glance side to side, they have an auditory bias. Therefore, eye contact is a significant factor in all interpersonal communication.

For example, the lack of direct eye contact during a conversation may suggest negativity or deception. At the same time, more consistent eye contact could indicate that someone is thinking more positively about what you are saying. Consistent eye contact may also mean that your conversational opponent does not trust you enough to take their eyes off you. If someone cannot look you directly in the eye, it may suggest they have something to hide. Whereas a resolute, hard, or blank facial expression may indicate some hostility towards you.

If your opponent is looking at you while using the arms across the chest barrier signal, your opponent's eye contact could be the deciding factor, suggesting that something is seriously bothering them about you and your message. If your words do not entirely convince your opponent, their attention and eyes may wander. In this case, their eyes will move away from contact with your own for extended periods compared to a normal engaged conversation. You have lost your audience. You probably talk too much, and they are bored with your words! Your opponent's boredom might also be indicated by their head tilting to one side or their eyes looking straight at you with a rested gaze in the 'middle-distance' area between you and them. If your opponent is excessively fiddling with something while looking at you during a conversation, it could also mean that their attention has drifted and is now fixed elsewhere. It could also mean that they are simply nervous. If your opponent is particularly interested in what you are saying, this might be indicated through posture, facial expressions, and extended eye contact. Conversely, if your opponent is deceitful, it can be displayed by excessive blinking and touching their face or lips in a masking gesture.

It is also worth considering that perhaps someone who expresses the typical signs of being anxious may have an anxiety disorder, a genuine medical condition. Therefore, they cannot make consistent eye contact without feeling significant personal discomfort. It is also worth noting that people with specific disabilities may use body language in a completely different way from others. In such circumstances, their level of disability, which may not be obvious, is also an essential factor to consider. In this instance, their body language cannot be appropriately factored into the overall assessment evaluation equation as it normally would. Furthermore, when dealing with people from different cultures, it is worth remembering that they may easily convey verbal and non-verbal communication in an entirely different way from what we accept as normal in Western society. Therefore, taking anything, including eye contact, as a stand-alone factor can be highly misleading.

The Mental Martial Artist's goal is to become an expert at accurately interpreting the meaning of other people's communications.

Another goal is to become an expert in conveying only the signals you wish to communicate to others. The Shaolin masters teach:

"Do not draw a universe from a single word, deed, or action."

Group Body Language

Your intimate space is particularly important and can be jealously guarded. No one genuinely appreciates its invasion unless it is invited. The approximations of an individual's personal space are as follows:

- 武 Intimate Space is closer than about 19 inches or 51 centimetres.
- 武 Social Space is about 5 feet or 1.5 metres.
- 武 Casual Space is anything between 5 and 10 feet or between 1.5 and 3 metres.

Therefore, if you are closer than an arm's reach to another person, you are technically inside that person's personal space. When people are in overcrowded spaces, they usually attempt to create more space automatically. To observe this in action, pay attention the next time you are on a crowded bus or the London Underground. You will notice that when someone invades a person's personal space, they will often become tense. They will also begin using their arms as subconscious forms of protection in various barrier positions. People in crowded situations will also try to avoid direct eye contact with those immediately around them. Taking the London Underground as an example, when a carriage is crowded, people will avoid making eye contact by staring at the same advertisement for minutes, reading it many times over. It makes this natural human instinct excellent news for those selling advertising space and those paying to advertise something!

When you enter a room full of people already engaged in group conversations, you have the opportunity to observe several forms of group body language. For instance, if the group is closed off and doesn't leave any opening for others to join, they are non-verbally signalling,

'Keep away; we don't want anyone interrupting our private conversation.' This underscores the importance of non-verbal communication in such situations, making you more aware and attentive. If two people are standing face-to-face, then this is a similar signal to that of the closed group signal. It is not easy or wise to attempt to break into such a conversation until they open up a little on their own. When they do, non-verbally, this would mean that it is OK for others to join the conversation if they wish. In this instance, they will probably be standing opposite each other in a non-direct position, such as an open V-shaped formation. Suppose a group in conversation is physically open, with individuals angled in several different directions. In that case, they communicate non-verbally that they are open to interruption and the intervention of others in the group.

These are just a few examples of what you typically encounter at networking events. Understanding these non-verbal cues can be the key to effective networking, potentially making the difference between a successful interaction and being perceived as a rude nuisance. This reiteration of the potential benefits should motivate you to learn more about body language in such events, making you more eager and proactive in your approach.

Chapter 5 Summary – Power Move:

武 *Unless you learn how to communicate the way others prefer to receive information, you are not communicating at all because they are simply not receiving your message.*

Chapter 5 Summary – Pressure Points:

武 *Communication somatotyping is an advanced technique to help you detect and decipher others' preferred communication biases.*

武 *The quality and power of your questions ultimately determine the quality of the information you will receive.*

Chapter 6: Conflict Resolution

Techniques for negotiating with difficult people and handling arguments are remarkably similar, so I will call both 'conflict' to make it easier.

Conflict can occur at any time, place, and in any aspect of your social, personal, or business life. In business, there is almost a constant low level of conflict because people are always trying to beat others to get promotions, pay raises, and increased status. Ego also plays a huge role in creating and then perpetuating corporate conflict. Some people in the corporate world seem to have an ego the size of Africa. These self-opinions are usually based on nothing except having an over-inflated opinion of themselves as a compensation mechanism to protect their fragile actual self-image. You can be sure that the bigger the person's ego is, the proportionally poorer self-image they will possess. There is the added complication of different personality types, which makes things even more interesting. Some people seem to enjoy being awkward, resistant, or just generally negative. Let us not forget the curmudgeons who offer nothing to others except rudeness and misery.

With all these variable factors and personalities to consider, conflict and arguments can occur for many reasons. Furthermore, most people allow themselves to be blindly drawn into a head-on conflict simply because they could not see it coming. Since there is such a high risk of conflict in so many different areas of your life, how should you approach it when it does arise? Furthermore, how do you effectively handle difficult people with a wide variety of personality types?

Concepts of Winning and Losing

There is one basic rule that will immediately help eliminate a great deal of conflict in your life. This is to learn how to recognise what a real contest is and what it is not. On the surface, this may appear to be both obvious and simple. However, in practice, it is usually much more difficult to assess. Most people almost habitually confuse things, and almost always seem to be in one worthless competition after another. I urge you to make a concerted effort to monitor yourself closely. When a potential competition scenario arises, ask yourself the following question: "Am I about to enter into a genuine competition, and if so, with whom?"

I am amazed by the number of people who view virtually everything in their lives as some ridiculous competition. Even the terminology they habitually use is associated with competition. For example, a guy might ask a friend if he 'scored' by dating a girl. While others might refer to it as being 'the dating game.' On the road, many drivers feel compelled to cut in front of another car to gain a worthless imaginary score over another driver.

When they did that, many shared that they felt better about gaining an additional 15 to 20 feet of distance compared to the car now behind them. Their fragile, flawed ego will not allow them to zipper-merge safely behind where there is plenty of room to spare. In airports worldwide, people waiting to board a flight go to extraordinary lengths to gain an extra few inches of space as they form a line to board a plane a few seconds ahead of someone else. From a sensible perspective, it is all ridiculous. Unfortunately, the list of pseudo-competitions many people enter daily could probably go on for several pages.

By engaging in pseudo-competitions such as these, you achieve nothing except wasting precious time and emotional energy on things without real meaning. Many people have deliberately allowed themselves to live most of their lives in a state of pseudo-competition. It is now a blind habit for them because it is all they know how to do. This situation eventually spells long-term disaster because it hugely debilitates all aspects of their life. Furthermore, everyone reading these words has almost certainly been drawn into a pseudo-conflict and competition at some point in life.

Almost everyone has been drawn into the parking space war at some point. Therefore, let us objectively examine the mechanisms behind all this. In doing so, you will also see how you can begin avoiding such negativity in the future. For example, you might be in a car park looking for a free space. Suddenly, you might spot one. However, someone else will beat you to it before you can reach it and park there. Imagine this scenario in detail. Visualise it clearly and examine how you feel and what emotions are generated as a result. If you were in this situation right now, would you feel you have lost in some way? Alternatively, would you completely ignore that someone else parked there ahead of you and drive on to find another space?

Do you let the simple fact that someone else parked ahead of you bother you so much that you become stressed and even angry about it? Do you feel compelled to stop and begin an argument with the other driver? If you are a man with a caveman-type intellect, would you feel that it may even be worth resorting to violence? How would you feel if you were trying to impress a new girlfriend who is in your car with you? Do you think she would be impressed if you behaved like a spoiled 6-year-old and either had a fight or performed an act of vandalism in revenge? There have even been extreme occasions when a similar scenario has resulted in the death of one party involved, with the other incarcerated for life. And all for what? A simple parking space...

When objectively considering these potential scenarios, I hope it has made you pause for a second to soul-search and question your typical response to that situation. Is your life so small that someone else taking a parking space ahead of you can generate worthless emotional reactions?

Surely, you must have other genuinely important things happening in your life to be concerned about. These reactions to someone else taking a car park place ahead of you all have one thing in common: they are worthless and waste time, energy, and effort. People can even end a long friendship over nothing more than a worthless pseudo-competition. I know because I have seen this happen.

For the following scenario, we have two fictional guys in a bar, Stuart and Paul. They are relaxing over a drink as they chat about their ability to attract women. Paul asks Stuart, "Did you score (score a date) with that girl last evening?" Stuart replies: "No, he didn't." However, he then reminds Paul that he did not 'score' either last evening when a similar opportunity presented itself. Subconsciously, both Paul and Stuart begin to see this as a contest, and neither party wishes to be the loser because they have their fragile egos at stake.

Paul then gloats while reminding Stuart of a previous time when he also 'failed to score.' Stuart immediately retaliates by making another cutting remark, attempting to counter the imaginary points being scored. This scenario could easily escalate into something more serious than a conversation as the two characters become locked in a pseudo-competition. I witnessed two people end a friendship for many years through this scenario. Their friendship ended over a ridiculous ego-driven pseudo-competition, which they should have grown out of before they reached their teenage years.

The next time you find yourself being drawn into a stupid pseudo-competition, please stop yourself and at least question what you are doing. Remember, your time, effort, and emotional energy are better spent on things that genuinely matter than on absolute nonsense. Furthermore, the people who typically waste their time this way usually do so because they do not have anything else of value to do in life. Surely, this is not you.

If you were in command of a military unit, would you commit them to fighting a battle based on nothing but imagination and ego? Almost certainly not. Recognising and then freeing yourself from worthless pseudo-competitions will free up your life, and you will have much more emotional energy to spare when facing the real challenges on the road to success.

Winning and Losing - The Misconceptions

There is a direct connection between pseudo-competitions and the often misguided concepts of winning and losing. I have always been fascinated by this concept. Words only possess whatever meaning and value we allow them to have. However, if we can define a value, a feeling, or an emotion associated with a word, then we can also change that value. Subconsciously, to some degree, we are all afraid of losing. Perhaps this is because it has been drummed into us from birth that winning is everything and losing is always bad. Therefore, if the word 'lose' is considered by many to be a negative word, how can we change the way we perceive and feel about it? To begin with, let us examine the feelings and emotions associated with the word. For example, think about the following phrases and how they make you feel:

- 武 I *lost* my job.
- 武 I *lost* my wallet.
- 武 I *lost* my girlfriend or boyfriend.
- 武 I *lost* my way.
- 武 I *lost* the freestyle combat.
- 武 I *lost* the contest.

In examining your feelings associated with those phrases, especially about the word 'lose,' your feelings were probably negative. You would not be alone in having those feelings; most people would feel the same as you do. However, is there ever a positive side to losing and the word 'lose'? As with all things in life, love, and business, there tends to be a balance. A Yin and a Yang complete the harmony and balance that nature insists upon. Therefore, there will always be a positive connotation to the concept of losing and the word 'lose.' If you want to begin changing the typical context, the associated emotions and typical feelings connected with losing to become something more neutral, then when you lose something, try adding a simple caveat in the following way:

- I *lost* my fear of interviews, and I got the job.
- I *lost* my wallet, but I was covered for double its contents by my insurance plan.
- I *lost* my girlfriend (or boyfriend), but it worked out well because I met someone new the same evening, and they are even more amazing!
- I *lost* my way, but it worked out well because I found a better route and a great new restaurant in the process.
- I *lost* the game, but I now realise my weak spots, which I need to work on, and we still won the overall tournament anyway.
- I *lost* the account, but this was the best thing that could have happened because that company announced bankruptcy the following week, leaving a string of creditors. Luckily, we avoided that by *losing* the account.

There is usually some upside to every event and scenario, even if it is not initially apparent. Removing your ego from the equation and learning to caveat positively, all the initial negative energy soon disappears. Now, let us examine the concept of winning. Once again, please explore the feelings and emotions associated with the word 'win' or 'winning.'

- I *won* the lottery.
- We *won* a huge contract for the company.
- We *won* the war.
- We *won* the lawsuit.
- I *won* his or her heart.
- I *won* the argument.

There is no doubt about it: the words and phrases about winning generate the opposite feelings and emotions of those associated with the word 'lose' or 'lost.' There is nothing wrong with winning; winning is always great, if you are in a legitimate contest. Please stop and think about that last line very carefully! Some things in life, love, and business are worth being in a contest for. However, many things are completely worthless, yet people still compete about them out of habit.

Remember, every experience in life, love, and business is merely data. It's up to you to decide whether it's good or bad. Similarly, it's your prerogative to categorise your perceptions and perspectives about winning and losing. This understanding of choice is a powerful tool in shaping your mindset.

Initiating a process of self-reflection on your feelings, perceptions, and perspectives associated with the concepts of winning and losing is the crucial first step in transforming them for the better. As you delve deeper into this self-exploration, you'll find that your feelings, perceptions, and perspectives start to shift. And as these changes take root, your responses to winning and losing will also evolve. With consistent practice over 21 days, this new response mechanism will solidify into a positive habit, bringing lasting benefits to your life. Quoting the great William Shakespeare:

"There is nothing either good or bad, but thinking makes it so."

It Takes All Kinds

Regarding conflict and conflict resolution, it is worth pausing to consider the different types of people you may have to engage as opponents. You may encounter people who enjoy putting you down at every opportunity. This is usually because, in doing so, they make themselves feel better. They enjoy being glacially sarcastic and speaking negatively about others at every opportunity.

You may also encounter what the military refers to as the 'UXB,' or the Unexploded Bomb. These people are an explosion of rage; they are just ready and waiting for a trigger, which allows them the excuse. When they find a suitable trigger, it can be sheer hell for anyone within their blast radius. Some are pressure people. These people think that applying constant and almost nagging pressure will better help them get their way. Such people go on and on, hoping to wear the other person down by pure attrition. While I could provide more examples, I'm confident that you can already think of several people who fit one or more of the above categories. Moreover, it's highly probable that you'll encounter many opponents with these characteristics in your career. So, how do you defend against such people? The answer is straightforward: stick to the principles of Mental Martial Arts. These principles are effective, and even adhering to a few can significantly impact your success or failure in handling conflicts.

- 武 Detach yourself emotionally and learn to become completely dispassionate in an engagement scenario.
- 武 Do not take anything personally; treat all communication and information as pure data.
- 武 Control your emotions and maintain a good emotional balance.
- 武 Always express the metaphorical shape of a sphere.
- 武 Always step out of the line of attacking energy.
- 武 Maintain an objective, strategic overview of the situation. As things change, so dispassionately factor in any new equations you are faced with.
- 武 You can either walk away or engage an opponent. It is always your choice, depending on the circumstances and the situation.
- 武 When you engage an opponent, blend your energy together. That way, you will take control of the engagement and the outcome.

By using these basic principles of Mental Martial Arts, all future engagement situations will cause you less distress and fewer problems. With practice, conflict situations will flow harmlessly around you.

Energy and Conflict Resolution

We have already established that all interactions in life, love, and business are simply an exchange of energy. Energy exchange and combat are handled similarly in physical martial arts and Mental Martial Arts. In martial arts, an imaginary energy line emanates from our body's central point outwards to others. Certain geometric shapes can metaphorically represent a different type of energy and the way that energy is both projected and received.

We can use these concepts to our advantage in dealing with conflict resolution. Imagine you are in a situation where someone is extremely angry with you. In this situation, they verbally send their angry energy flow straight down their centre energy line, directly into your centre. What do you do about it? Do you stay in line with your opponent's angry energy, constantly retreating in the hope that it will somehow dissipate while gathering your thoughts and considering what to do next? By staying in line with an attack and continually trying to deflect attacks while retreating, you are absorbing both the attack and the negative energy. This does not work very well. Furthermore, when you are under pressure from an attack like this, you may be tempted to react instead of responding, which is also not particularly good.

Since logic rarely changes an emotion, if someone is angry with you, no matter how much you reason with them logically and try to counter their angry energy, it will not help very much. The last thing you want is to become engaged in a scenario where you feel compelled to retaliate with petty remarks to relieve some of the pressure you are feeling from the attack. What is the better way of dealing with an attack like this?

To help me describe a better way to deal with an attack like this, I will use the analogy of a physical martial artist in a combat scenario. Since a martial artist would typically respond to an attack and never react, they would first remove themselves from the direct line of the attack by stepping sideways, not backwards. The martial artist would then physically connect with their opponent's attacking limb, with the limb representing their attacking energy.

This is because unless they engage their opponent and make contact, it will be more challenging for them to resolve the situation. If they do not, their attacker's limb and energy are still available to launch new attacks. Once they successfully engage their opponent, the attacking energy can be neutralised and guided to the desired outcome. When engaging with the attack, the more physically aligned they become with the attacking energy, the easier it is to deal with. This is simple physics. A highly skilled martial artist may even be able to use an opponent's attacking energy against them, making their attacker self-destructive.

The Mental Martial Artist would seek to do the same metaphorically, and the rules of engagement are the same as if you are being physically attacked. Always respond, and never react. Remember that everything you see and hear is merely data you will then categorise appropriately and objectively. You will also remove your ego from the equation, and in doing so, you will redefine the traditional concepts of winning and losing.

You will metaphorically engage your attacker just as a physical martial artist would engage the attacking limb of their opponent. You will then try to align your energy with that of your opponent. Just like the physics of dealing with a physical attack, which makes it easier to deal with when your energy is aligned, the same is true of a metaphoric attack. Once you have engaged the opponent and aligned your energy with your attacker, you can begin guiding and directing the energy.

Once you begin guiding the energy, your objective is to neutralise it as you guide the engagement to your desired conclusion. Naturally, a Mental Martial Artist would not physically engage an attacker; instead, you will engage your opponent using carefully chosen words and phrases. Strategically using communication skills, body language skills, and other methods we have touched upon, the words and phrases you use will help you to neutralise the attack. They will also help align yourself with your attacker's energy as you do so. The Mental Martial Artist's goal is to make initial contact using blending and harmonising words and phrases such as:

- 武   I fully understand you.
- 武   I completely understand your perspective.
- 武   I might feel the same way about the information you are using.

(There are several more ideas about 'blending' words and phrases in the section on communication.)

One of the greatest masters of the physical martial arts, Morihei Ueshiba, the founder of Aikido, once said that you should be prepared to "stare death in the face" before committing to your move. In Mental Martial Arts, you often must do the same metaphorically. In principle, the more powerful and direct the attacking line of energy becomes, the easier it is to handle. The slower and more calculated an attack becomes, the greater the skill and proficiency needed to deal with it. Engaging your attacker at the very last moment, when your opponent is absolutely committed to their move, makes it extremely difficult to change the direction of their attack. From that point onwards, once you have re-aligned and blended your position with that of your opponent, you will begin to take control of the engagement.

Bridging

Bridging is connecting two things to form a common link. Similarly, to align the perspectives of two people who are often in complete opposition, metaphoric 'bridges' must be built. These bridges are comprised of words and phrases which are designed to build emotional connections with your opponent. They show that you understand them and their perspective and that you genuinely wish to resolve matters in a way that they will probably be happy with. This understanding, this empathy, is the key to successful bridging.

The bridging technique is something that journalists use in interviews and debates when they are attempting to back politicians into a corner. Bridging removes you from the direct line of your opponent's attack, and at the same time, it forms your first connection with them. In other words, you have successfully engaged your opponent. As you are subtly guiding the conversation, you should always choose words and phrases that will make your opponent feel as though you are becoming increasingly aligned with their point of view. I have listed some typical bridging words and phrases that will serve as an acknowledgement of what your opponent has said and allow you to connect with them in a bridging form. Initially, they may appear to be much like the list of engaging words and phrases in the previous section, but they are not. They are a much more advanced technique. Rest assured, with practice, you will master this technique and feel secure in your ability to resolve conflicts effectively.

- That isn't quite the issue...
- Let's not forget that...
- The most important thing is...
- You may say that, however...
- I don't think that is so important...

Now that you have engaged your opponent and removed yourself from the direct line of attack, carefully choose words and phrases that suggest that you understand your opponent and might even feel the same way they do. Here are some examples.

- The 'XYZ' product or company is excellent...
- It sounds as though you know what you are talking about...
- You can obviously see things clearly...
- It appears you understand the market, the concept, or the product...

At this point in the engagement, your opponent should at least begin to feel as though you understand them. This also creates a little confusion in your opponent. This is because it is almost certain that they would assume you would resist them head-on, so they will be ready for an argument you are not giving them. Instead, your action of immediately diffusing, bridging, and blending with them will have taken them by surprise. Next, you can increase your control over the engagement by using more advanced Mental Martial Arts techniques. You may consider using more leading or even loaded questions.

There is a big difference between a leading question and a loaded question. A leading question will have a subtle bias designed to suggest, insinuate, or solicit a specific answer. Such a question is designed to lead your opponent to confirm certain information in their answer. For example, a leading question would be: "Were you at the Apollo Gym exercising on Thursday evening, the 6th of June?" This question contains the suggestion that your opponent was at a specific location on the day in question. The same question, composed in a non-leading format, would be: "Where were you on Thursday evening, June 6th?"

A loaded question is different because it contains an unjustified assumption or presumption. For example, a loaded question would be: "Have you stopped taking illegal anabolic steroids?" No matter what your opponent answers, either yes or no, the suggestion has been made that they have already admitted to taking illegal anabolic steroids. In this way, the fact is presupposed by how the question has been phrased. This technique often narrows your opponent's response to a single answer. Even if some injunction or justification follows the answer, it carries much less impact because you have highlighted a presupposed fact.

Why?

Why is 'why?' such a powerful question? The question 'Why?' comprises what is broadly termed as Socratic Questioning, which originates from the great ancient Greek philosopher Socrates. This question can be used to probe concepts, issues, problems, incidents, principles, and even theories. It is also an excellent way to help you understand precisely what and how your opponent thinks. Since no one can object to polite and well-phrased enquiring questions, it makes it difficult for your opponent not to reveal more than they might otherwise wish to. For example, the 'why?' question could be used and phrased as follows:

- 武 **To clarify thinking – Question:** 'Why do you say that? Could you please explain in more detail?'
- 武 **To question your opponent's question – Question:** 'Why do you think the question is important? Why do you think I asked you that question?'
- 武 **To Challenge your opponent – Question:** 'Is this always the way? Please tell me why you think the assumption you make is valid?'
- 武 **To implicate and imply consequence – Question:** 'If X happened, what would be the result? How would X Affect Y?'
- 武 **As evidence for or against your opponent – Question:** 'Why do you say that? Is there any possible doubt about your data?'
- 武 **To suggest an alternative – Question:** 'What could the argument be against X?

So long as you are polite in your approach, you can continue to ask 'why?' as often as needed. Supporting the question with appropriately loaded and leading questions is a good idea. These will help your opponent to talk themselves into the belief or position that you wish them to take. These techniques are excellent for getting right to the point and countering an opponent so that it will eventually wear them down.

It is like a practitioner of Kung Fu who uses a technique called 'limb destruction' when countering the attack of an opponent. If you remember, limb destruction occurs when an attacker delivers a strike, and the defending martial artist counters it so that the defending block is targeted at a nerve point on the attacking limb. Using this method, when a strike is made against you, each blocking action you make does not just defend you against being hit; it also delivers a nasty attack to your opponent. In other words, whenever they try to hurt you, they hurt themselves even more. Eventually, this process wears them down and decreases your attacker's ability to attack you.

Here are some examples of words and phrases you can use to first engage with, then bridge with, and then redirect the attacking energy flow of your opponent.

Engage Your Opponent and Acknowledge.	Bridge to Blend and Re-direct the Energy Flow.	Redirect the Energy Accordingly.
I'm glad you asked that question.	Redirect the energy flow.	*Thanks for reminding me...*
Good question.	Redirect the energy flow.	*As we know/agree...*
Good Point.	Redirect the energy flow.	*Thanks for helping me clear this up...*
Thanks for reminding me.	Redirect the energy flow.	*As you said earlier...*
Thanks for helping make this clear.	Redirect the energy flow.	*We all appreciate your help...*
That isn't quite the issue.	Redirect the energy flow.	*I/we believe...*
I don't know that.	Redirect the energy flow.	*What I do know is...*
Let's not forget that.	Redirect the energy flow.	*The Key Issues are...*
That isn't quite right.	Redirect the energy flow.	*Why I say that is...*

You may say that, however.	Redirect the energy flow.	*Equally important is/are...*
I don't think that is so important.	Redirect the energy flow.	*What is Important, however, is...*
That isn't quite correct.	Redirect the energy flow.	*Let me explain...*
I/we don't believe that..	Redirect the energy flow.	*What I/we do believe, however,*

Engage Your Chi Emotional Intelligence

Before you can engage your emotional intelligence, you must first become conscious of it. Once you have become conscious of it, you can learn how to use and engage it. This will be the equivalent of putting your finger on the metaphoric pulse of everything that is happening in your life. It is widely recognised that emotional intelligence, in the generally accepted sense, is the ability to identify, assess, and control your emotions and those of others you interact with. I would also like to make it clear that I am not in any way alluding to the classical Darwinian model of emotional intelligence. Naturally, in principle, the instinct of survival and adaptation are interconnected at a base level within all of us.

I refer to Chi's emotional intelligence as all of the above plus the cultivation of the little-used and often-overlooked senses within all of us. In most people, these senses usually remain dormant or have not been developed to their fullest potential in others. A martial arts master would also use what is commonly referred to as their Chi. Therefore, an integral component of Chi's emotional intelligence is developing a highly developed and refined awareness. When you eventually achieve this state, you should be able to detect the slightest change in the energy, feeling, and atmosphere of everyone you encounter.

With practice, when you sense such a move or a shift in others, you should then be able to assess and predict the associated repercussions. Once you have initially heightened your senses in this way, you should be able to make it part of what you do automatically at a subconscious level. At this point, it will almost be like you can make an accurate prediction based entirely on the evidential factors and data you receive. To other people, this same information remains completely unnoticed or, at best, appears completely unconnected. Sir Arthur Conan Doyle extensively discussed a similar technique in his books about the great detective Sherlock Holmes. Those familiar with his works will remember how Holmes could detect the slightest movement and changes to the infinitely delicate criminal web of his arch-villain, Professor Moriarty. Holmes could always clearly envision the multi-layer cause-and-effect mechanism of every change, no matter how small. This was usually to the amazement of his ever-faithful companion, Dr Watson.

The physical martial artist will probably immediately recognise this technique as Chi Sau (pronounced Chee Sow) or Sticking Hands. In Chi Sau practice, two people would engage each other at the wrist with half-extended arms. At this point, the two would be relaxed, engaging each other with only minimal pressure on the wrists. Both would then start to gently move in a slight rolling motion of the arms, and in doing so, they explore potential weaknesses in their opponent's defence. The object of the exercise is to feel and sense the very slightest pressure or tension in their opponent and respond accordingly.

Sometimes, it might be a combination of the tension of an arm muscle and an associated eye movement, which might signal what their opponent would do next. Additional factors considered would include breathing, stance, and foot movements. When combined with the data received from the contact between the arms, an objective and predictive sense will become clear. It is then possible to detect the slightest differences between a feint and an actual strike. Then, it becomes possible to be predicatively prepared to counter the move. If executed correctly and at a high level, two art experts would never break the motion. Instead, they would perform a continuous series of flowing moves and counter-movements.

The challenge for the student of the Mental Martial Artist is to apply this concept in daily life, love, and business. With practice, this is not nearly as difficult as it may at first appear, despite many more data elements to be considered. The secret to success in this technique is to view all things completely dispassionately and only as data. Never take anything personally, and keep an open mind. With practice, you will soon find that this technique will allow you to stay one step ahead of others. Furthermore, you will begin to understand more than you ever thought possible about what is happening around you at any moment. Quote:

"Use only the minimum force when engaging an opponent; however, use extraordinary force to strike the winning blow."

Controlling Your Emotional Expression

Let's take the hypothesis that all people express metaphoric shapes directly linked to their emotional state and expressed energy. It also follows that you must become increasingly aware of your emotional state and the metaphoric shape you express to others around you. To do this, you first need to become more in tune with your emotions and feelings and practice being objectively dispassionate. However, I am not suggesting for one moment that you should aim to become an emotionless being like Mr Spock in Star Trek. However, I am suggesting that you learn to control your emotions. Here are some suggestions which will help you achieve better control.

Do not be afraid of your feelings and emotions. Emotions and feelings are nothing more than sensory feedback from your body, allowing you to 'feel' as a human being. Emotions and feelings give us a wide variety of sensations, including fear, anger, love, etc.; sometimes, some take us by surprise. Everyone has feelings and emotions, and people who repress them are not being strong; instead, they are repressing them because they are weak. To learn how to control your emotions, you first must embrace, express, and accept them. Relax your normally well-restrained self, and when in private, allow yourself to shout, jump around and do things that you would typically not allow yourself to do. Taking a few acting classes is also an excellent way to familiarise yourself with your feelings and emotions and help you learn how to express and control them effectively. Concerning acting, another easy way to help you control your emotions and feelings is to roleplay a character who can deal with a situation similar to the one you are facing. You may even wish to portray a movie character you have seen onscreen who possesses the ideal qualities you desire.

The next step is understanding the difference between your feelings and emotions. Since emotions and feelings create a range of different physical manifestations, learning to understand your emotions will help you begin to understand the differences. Make a mental note of how each physical manifestation affects you and what triggers the emotions that produce them.

Exercise your emotions to build up an emotional reserve of strength, as you would strengthen your body to prepare for participation in sport. Ensure you get enough sleep, good nutrition, and a healthy time with your friends and family. It would be best if you also practice controlling your emotions and feelings. When you next begin to experience a strong emotion, pause for a second and breathe deeply. Then, ask yourself where you are physically feeling this. When you identify where you may want to touch that area physically, you affirm that what you are experiencing is nothing more than energy. Breath control will help you to control this process, just as proper breathing is essential when practising martial arts. This should help alleviate many annoying physical manifestations, such as feeling a 'lump' in your throat or a 'knot' in your stomach. Practising this process regularly will help you use it more easily when you need it the most. It will also help you release any negative energy more easily when it builds up.

Visualising Metaphysical Shapes and Expressions

Effective general visualisation will help you better envision the specific metaphysical shapes and energy they express. To express an outward metaphysical signature that is always calm, relaxed, adaptive, and responsive, you should always try to envision yourself as being and expressing the qualities of a sphere. This will allow you to effectively deal with the attacking words, energy, emotions, and feelings of others. A sphere will naturally roll easily and adapt; it will also naturally deflect attacks because it does not ever really offer an attacker a surface that can absorb an attack. This should always be your natural metaphysical envisioned shape. To help you better visualise this expression, try thinking about how a ball moves in a pinball machine or how the Dyson ball vacuum cleaner can freely move in almost any direction. Learning to control your emotions and express the right metaphysical shape takes patience and practice. Building on these ideas, I will explore this concept concerning conflict and conflict resolution more strategically.

In an energy exchange between two people, there is a metaphysical energy line between them. Each of these energy lines expresses a metaphysical shape. A Mental Martial Artist would be expressed as a sphere, while their opponent may express a variety of different shapes. If the Mental Martial Artist is attacked verbally, the angry person's expressed shape becomes slightly edgy and aggressive. They also direct aggressive, arrow-shaped energy to the Mental Martial Artist. The Mental Martial Artist will then metaphorically easily roll sideways and forwards, out of the attacking energy line and towards the attacker. Their conversation will blend, guide, and redirect the attacking energy as they do so. Eventually, when the energy has been aligned, the metaphoric shape of the attacker will also change to something less aggressive. Furthermore, because the energy of both parties has now been realigned, they will take the larger metaphoric shape of the corner bases of a triangle. The direction of the newly aligned energy flow will then be directed towards the apex of the triangle.

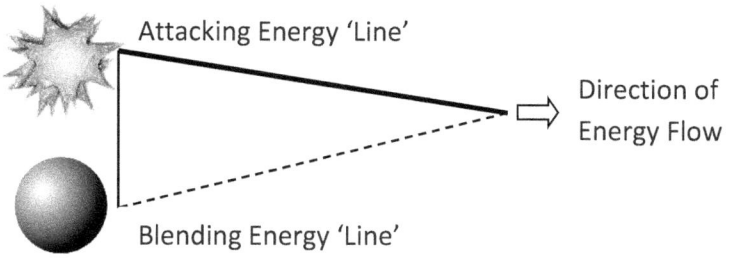

As the Tai Chi masters say:

"Respond only to the aggressive force, and then only 4 ounces can deflect a weight of 1,000 pounds."

Countdown and Checklist to an Engagement

If you believe that an engagement with an opponent cannot be avoided, here is a recap of some vital points that you can use to form your checklist before an engagement.

- 武 Completely remove your ego from the engagement; otherwise, it will interfere with your good sense.
- 武 Control your emotions. Pausing and breathing deeply will help you remain calm even in extremely difficult situations.
- 武 Do not take anything personally; all the information you receive is nothing more than data.
- 武 Ask as many questions as you feel appropriate. Your strategy and response are based on data, so you are only as good as the quality of your questions because they will be determined by the data you receive.
- 武 Seek to gain as much intelligence about your opponent as possible before an engagement. Anything will be of help, especially learning why they might have a different perspective than you do.
- 武 Make sure that all your data is accurate. Even if your opponent does not have all their data collated or correct, it is their problem.

You always should, and if you do not, it will undermine your credibility.

- Timing is an essential ingredient for success in any engagement. Without good timing in physical martial arts, you would be clumsy and ineffective. The same is true in Mental Martial Arts.
- Patience is a virtue, especially when engaging an opponent, because it can help you to win!
- Learn to always respond and never react. You must always remain dispassionate.
- Remember, it is not a competition where you must win every point. As Sir Winston Churchill knew well, winning every battle was not important; winning the overall war was the main objective.
- Never confuse activity with accomplishment. This is extremely easy to do, especially when reacting to a situation rather than responding.
- Always choose your ground to engage your opponent rather than let them dictate where it will be. A physical martial artist would do the same. They would never choose to engage an opponent from a disadvantaged position.
- If your opponent is more powerful than you are, then your natural advantage is in speed and manoeuvrability, so catch them off guard. Plan your strategy to ensure your opponent does not know exactly where and how to defend from your tactical advances.
- When engaging an opponent who is highly skilled at defence, it is essential to seem to be formless, nebulous, and almost invisible to your opponent.

Always appear to be strong and never show any signs of weakness. This gives you a distinct psychological advantage over your opponent, and you will have them constantly second-guessing themselves.

They may even come to fear you in some way. There is an old proverb that says, "Fear of death is worse than death itself." The same is true metaphorically in Mental Martial Arts.

Your power and strength may be nothing more than an illusion to your opponent; however, your opponent's perception of you is always their reality.

- 武 Lead your opponent into making mistakes and false moves. This causes your opponent to waste precious time, energy, and resources. Lead your opponent into reacting rather than responding to your moves and changes in tactics. Lure your opponent into making worthless moves by creating the illusion that they will gain a false advantage.
- 武 Constantly destabilise your opponent, and then, at the point before they regain stability, destabilise them again. This will generate a constant feeling of discomfort and confusion in your opponent. With good timing, your destabilised opponent may never actually regain their stability.
- 武 Ensure that your opponent is weighed down by as much process, red tape, and paperwork as possible. At the same time, you should always seek to retain your responsive flexibility and freedom of movement. This will help you create an advantage while constantly weakening your opponent.

Engaging a Single Opponent

In the following example scenarios, I will explore how to engage single and then multiple opponents using text and tactical diagrams. The characters should be familiar to almost everyone: a factious Sales Manager and Vice President of Sales (VP).

VP of Sales: *"I'm not very happy with your sales figures."*
(A direct attack)

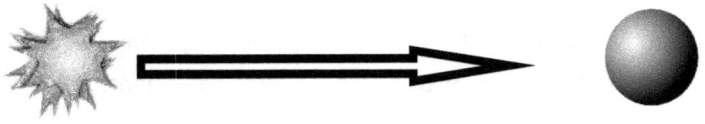

VP of Sales	Attacking Energy 'Line'	Sales Manager

Sales Manager: *"I don't blame you."*

(The Sales Manager moves aside, out of the attacking energy line, to begin aligning and blending their Chi energy with that of the attacker)

VP of Sales	Attacking Energy 'Line'	*The Sales Manager steps sideways, out of the attacking energy line.*

VP of Sales: *"You don't blame me?!"*

(The attacker is now confused and destabilised.)

Sales Manager: *"I wouldn't blame anybody for feeling the way that you do. It's obvious that you're not happy, and I can't argue with that..."*

(The Sales Manager engages the attacker.)

VP of Sales: *"But, do you really think that your work is up to standard?"*

(Confusion increases in the VP of Sales, and the destabilisation of the attacker continues to increase.)

Sales Manager: *"It can't be what you expect if you're not happy. My job is to sell our product; that's what you hired me for."*

(The Sales Manager continues to align and blend their Chi energy while engaged with the opponent. This creates more thinking time to evaluate the situation.)

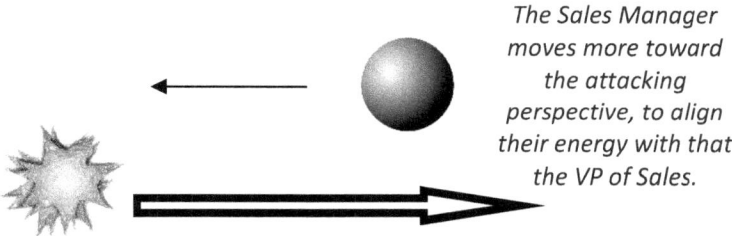

The Sales Manager moves more toward the attacking perspective, to align their energy with that the VP of Sales.

VP of Sales   Attacking Energy 'Line'

VP of Sales: *"But, I don't understand..."*

(The attacking VP of sales is now very confused and has not regained stability.)

Sales Manager: *"If you don't think that I should be fired outright, then let's work together to find a solution which is good for both of us. Tell me about some of your thoughts."*

(The Sales Manager now starts leading the engagement and redirects the energy of the attacker.)

VP of Sales: *"Well, it's your closing that's not strong enough. It seems like you could close more sales."*

(The VP of Sales' attacking energy begins to soften and become more aligned and blended with that of the Sales Manager.)

Sales Manager: *"Every salesperson closes in their unique way, which works best for them. However, if you give me an example of what you are looking for me to do, then I'll do exactly that. Was there anything else you wanted to discuss?"*

(The engagement is now being controlled by the Sales Manager. The energy and outcome of the attack are now being guided toward the Sales Manager's desired outcome.)

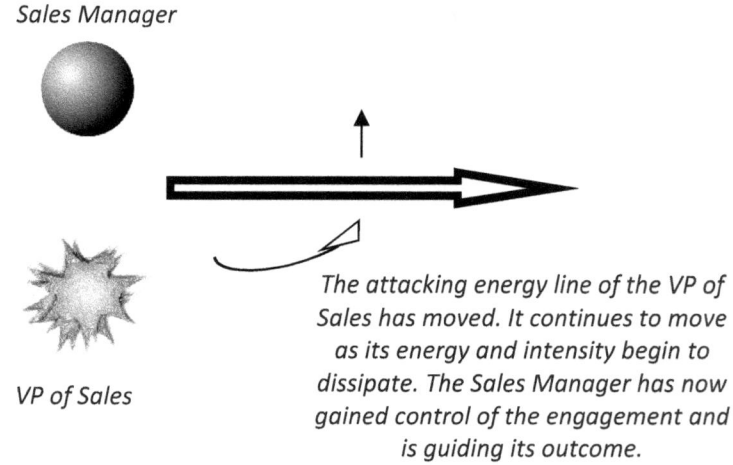

The attacking energy line of the VP of Sales has moved. It continues to move as its energy and intensity begin to dissipate. The Sales Manager has now gained control of the engagement and is guiding its outcome.

VP of Sales: *"Well, I suppose I might have overreacted a little. I'm sorry I was so blunt. I've had the end-of-month presentation looming up, and it's been bothering me a great deal. It must have seemed like you were under attack for no reason. Actually, your sales figures are OK."*

(The attack has been diffused. The VP of Sales feels as if they won the engagement and feels better understood by the Sales Manager.)

Sales Manager

VP of Sales

Attacking energy 'Line' is now diffusing into nothing, as if the engagement had never happened.

Sales Manager: *"I completely understand. I imagine that life at the top can be incredibly challenging at times."*

(Chi energy alignment has now been blended and restored, with harmony being the result.)

VP of Sales: *"You're right about that. Have a wonderful evening, and I'll see you tomorrow."*

(The VP of Sales now feels good about the Sales Manager and quite possibly slightly guilty for being too tough for no good reason.)

Sales Manager

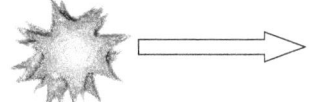

VP of Sales

The Chi Energy line of both parties is now completely aligned. The two parties are once again in harmony, with united energy flowing in the same common direction.

This scenario was a simple yet excellent example of engaging an attacker and redirecting the attacking energy to reach your desired outcome. Mental Martial Arts will often provide the opportunity to achieve a win-win outcome in this way. However, the attacker will usually feel like they have won the engagement, even though you gave them their supposed victory. More importantly, you will have achieved your desired outcome from the engagement. Therefore, it does not matter if the other person openly feels like they have won. It is far better to allow your opponent to believe this than to remain in a fruitless conflict, hoping you may eventually win in another way. Proving you are a winner is nothing more than a worthless expression of ego. Allowing your opponent the possibility of a win-win outcome to an engagement will cost you nothing and open the door to a more productive future relationship if you remove your ego from the equation. To quote the Shaolin Masters:

"Being the creator of your enemy will ultimately see you become the creator of your downfall."

Engaging Multiple Attackers

Engaging multiple attackers is a situation where you are engaged with two attackers working against you together. It may surprise you that a scenario where you are engaged with multiple attackers can be easier to handle than dealing with a single attacker. However, even the thought of a scenario where you are pitted against more than one opponent may be quite alarming to many people. This is because, from an early age, we are generally taught to think in the following terms:

- 武 The more, the better.
- 武 The bigger, the stronger.
- 武 The more troops, ships, and planes that the armed forces have, the better the armed forces are.

There are many more examples I could include. However, I am sure that you understand my point. I will examine some of these concepts in the context of engaging with multiple opponents while still emerging victorious. In the process, some of the points listed above will be revealed as nothing more than illusions. Taking my own country of birth as an example, British imperial history is littered with countless incidents where a technically inferior native army defeated a well-trained and heavily armed regiment of soldiers. This example is far from unique. Almost all countries' military histories, from Vietnam to the Middle East, have similar stories. An excellent example happened in 1879 during the Zulu War in South Africa. A Zulu army of over 20,000 warriors wiped out a heavily armed British regiment of 1,300 troops at the Battle of Isandlwana. Despite the inferior numbers of the British regiment, they should have been victorious because of their technology and superior firepower. However, they were not for many reasons, mostly involving abysmal leadership. These unexpected outcomes challenge our preconceived notions, questioning the conventional wisdom of military victories.

We have also been conditioned over the years to believe that defeat is almost always inevitable when facing many opponents at one time. This is not always the case. Consider modern warfare and the comparatively small but immensely powerful regiment of the British Army, the Special Air Service, or SAS. For those unfamiliar with their background, the SAS was technically the world's first modern special forces. They were formed in 1941 during the North African Campaign against a man who was arguably Adolf Hitler's finest general, Field Marshall Erwin Rommel, aptly nicknamed 'The Desert Fox.' The job of the SAS was to support Field Marshall Montgomery's 8th Army, better known as the 'Desert Rats', by carrying out what we know today as Special Forces operations behind enemy lines. They were so successful at this task that they played a significant role in Rommel's defeat.

Since the SAS was formed, they have proven on many occasions that small, highly trained Special Forces units are extremely effective. They were proven so good that many other countries decided to follow suit. America's Delta Force was formed in 1979 by Colonel Charles Beckwith, who served with 22 Regiment SAS as an exchange officer. He recognised the urgent need for a similar unit in the United States Armed

Services. The SAS regiment today comprises a comparatively small number of troops, yet they have proven themselves vastly superior to larger forces on many occasions. They have been highly successful in many wars, such as the Gulf War, the Iraq War, and the Falklands War, as well as successfully rescuing the hostages from the London Iranian Embassy siege in 1980. In short, bigger is not always better.

Let's now consider the SAS and highly trained martial artists as prime examples. One person can engage and defeat multiple opponents with the proper training and mindset. A scenario where you might face multiple opponents could easily occur in your workplace. The key to handling such a situation is to engage only one opponent at a time. As a rule, engage the attacker you believe will be the easiest to handle and defeat. This strategy allows you to focus your energy and resources effectively, increasing your chances of success. In Mental Martial Arts terms, this might be the attacker you believe was the easiest to win over to your way of thinking. You will find that there will always be one stronger attacker in almost every scenario where you are engaging multiple attackers. Once you have identified who this is, engage the weaker of the two attackers. On the rare occasions when both attackers are equal in strength, choose to engage with whom your instinct believes will be the easiest to deal with first.

Follow the Mental Martial Arts rules of engaging an opponent precisely as in the previous example. Once you have begun aligning and blending your energy with one of your opponents, you should seek to set that attacker into conflict with the other attacker. It is usually easiest to place the weaker of your two opponents into conflict with the stronger one. Do this by creating conflict between the two attackers, which will divide them, dilute their energy, confuse them, and eventually conquer them. This makes it easier to deal with the stronger attacker because the weaker one has already done some of the work for you. In this example scenario, imagine you are called Stuart; unbeknownst to you, you are about to be attacked. Attacker 1 is called Andy, and Attacker 2 is named Bill. The engagement might go something like this.

Andy: "Hey, Stuart, Bill and I don't like the way you've been running the gym when it's your shift of work. The paperwork's never been completed in the way you know I prefer, and Bill always seems to be left with more trial members to coach than you do."

(A double attack, as Andy leads Bill against you, as the imaginary character, Stuart.)

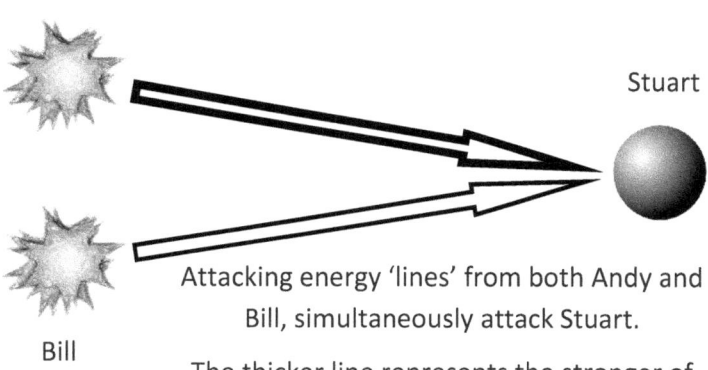

Attacking energy 'lines' from both Andy and Bill, simultaneously attack Stuart.

The thicker line represents the stronger of the two attacks.

Bill: "Yeah, that's right. Andy and I are getting sick of you not pulling your weight."

(Bill reinforces Andy's attack and expresses his frustration at the same time.)

Stuart: "Guys, I have to say that I'd probably agree with you. I believe that I'd feel the same as you do if roles were reversed. However, Andy always told me that you (Bill) really enjoy taking the beginners on their trial sessions. Since that's what you enjoy, I wanted to give you more of the fun stuff. Besides, you're just so good at it. You are a 'natural' with beginners. You make them feel so much more at ease than I do. Andy, remember when you told me that?"

(Stuart has engaged Bill and immediately makes him feel good about himself. This begins the process of alignment and blending of their energy and their perspectives. Stuart suggested that Andy once said

complimentary things about Bill, and even if he cannot remember saying it, he would probably not deny it. This has started to place Bill and Andy in conflict with each other, in a confusion of 'who said what, and when', etc.)

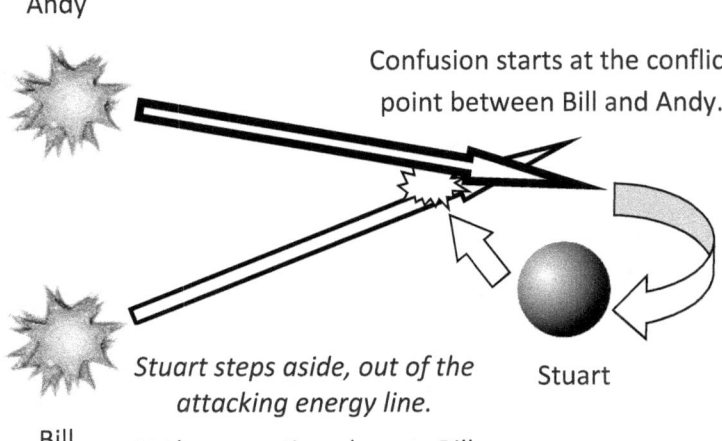

Confusion starts at the conflict point between Bill and Andy.

Stuart steps aside, out of the attacking energy line.

At the same time, he sets Bill, the weaker of the two attackers, into conflict with Andy.

Bill: *"Did you really say that, Andy? Did you tell Stuart that I enjoyed taking the beginners on their trial sessions and that I was particularly good at it?"*

(Unwittingly being led by Stuart, Bill is entering into conflict with Andy. However, Bill's ego is being bolstered because of the praise; this serves to slightly dilute his negative energy as he seeks positive reinforcement of his skills.)

Andy: *"Well, yes, actually, I did say that, after all, you are very good at handling new clients."*

(Confusion continues to grow, and Andy is diluting his attacking energy by thinking about what he remembers telling Stuart about Bill and not about his original objective.)

Stuart: *"Andy, you know that I'm learning a lot about the job from you; you're a great coach and a great role model. Since you are so good at the paperwork, excellent, in fact, perhaps you could coach me to be better at that. Bill, I also remember you telling me something about the last shift of the day and that I didn't always have to clean up* *at that time because we always had cleaning crews working overnight?"*

(After weakening the attack by engaging Bill, the weaker of the two attackers, Stuart is now aligning and blending his energy with both Andy and Bill. Stuart now seeks to fully align and blend his energy with Andy, so he also extends genuine compliments to appeal to Andy's ego. This technique further dilutes the attack, and it increases the confusion between Andy and Bill about what the initial objective of their attack was.)

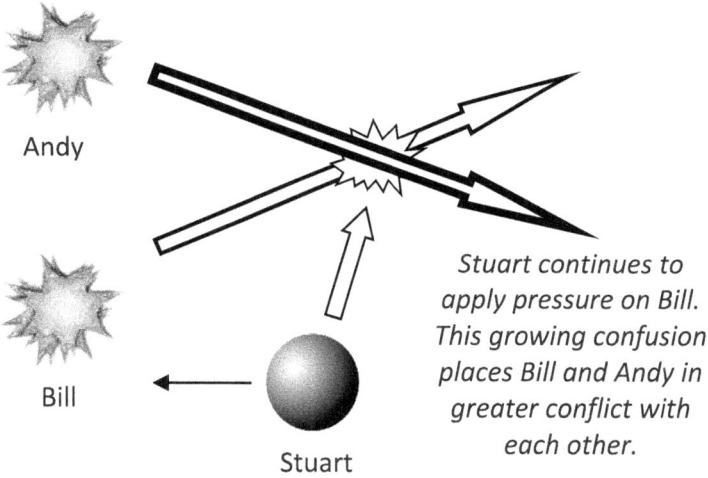

Stuart continues to apply pressure on Bill. This growing confusion places Bill and Andy in greater conflict with each other.

This technique continues to destabilise both Andy and Bill's combined attack.

At the same time, Stuart continues to move towards blending and aligning his own energy, initially with Bill, and then with both Bill and Andy together.

Bill: *"Well, I suppose that we do have cleaning crews overnight, but only on weekdays, not on weekends. Andy should have told you about that."*

(Stuart is now leading Bill's energy and perspective while he still maintains a conflict situation between Bill and Andy.)

Stuart: *"You're right, Bill. I know we all agree with you. I also know that I can learn a lot about the job from you, especially from how expertly you handle the new members. They always enjoy your induction sessions; Andy once mentioned that to me."*

(Stuart is further strengthening his blended energy with Bill. His sincere compliments directed at Bill continue to lead his energy into diffusion, while at the same time, Stuart begins the harmonisation process between Andy and Bill.)

Andy: *"Actually, Stuart, I don't mind coaching you on the paperwork, especially if it helps us all. Do you really think that I'm that good at it? I never considered myself to be that good at the sales paperwork; I suppose I must be."*

(Stuart is now leading Andy to a calm conclusion by blending and aligning both of their energies.)

Bill: *"Hey, Stuart, if you'd like, we can work out a better rota together for the late shift and the tidy-up sessions. Maybe I'll share a tip or two with you in the process about why I'm so good with beginners!"*

(Bill is now calm, with his energy blended and aligned with Stuart.)

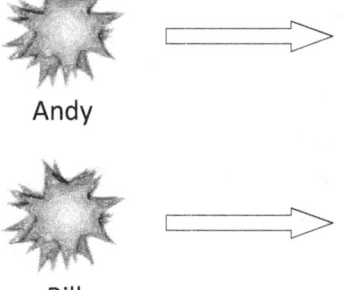

Stuart has fully aligned and blended his Chi Energy with that of both Andy, and Bill.

The combined attack was diffused by Stuart placing Andy and Bill into conflict, and confusion against each other. Thus, placing Stuart in control of the engagement.

Stuart then re-aligned and blended all three energy channels and perspectives.

Now all are friends again, after a win-win conclusion has been achieved.

That was a simple example of how to engage multiple attackers using several new techniques, including:

- 武 Engaging the weaker of the two attackers first.
- 武 How to cross-confuse an opponent by placing the attackers into conflict with each other.
- 武 Leading, suggesting what has been said and implying what has been agreed.

Remember, the principle is the same no matter how many attackers are involved in the engagement. First, divide the enemy, confuse them, and set them in conflict with each other.

Also, remember that in some instances, you will find it easier to create confusion and conflict if you have a larger number of opponents. To summarise, the key points of handling conflict and conflict resolution with difficult people are:

- 武 Listen carefully to your opponent.
- 武 Remove your ego from the equation.
- 武 All information received is data, nothing more.
- 武 Eliminate the traditional concepts of winning and losing from the equation.
- 武 Observe all things from a tactical perspective.
- 武 Choose your ground carefully and make your moves from there.
- 武 Choose your timing carefully.
- 武 Step out of the direct line of attack.
- 武 Blend and align your Chi energy with that of your opponent while also creating conflict between the multiple attackers.
- 武 Always remain engaged with your opponent and maintain your Chee Sau or *finger on the pulse* of what is happening.
- 武 Take control of the energy and the differing perspectives in the engagement.
- 武 Lead the direction of the engagement.
- 武 If possible, conclude the engagement with a 'win-win' scenario.

Chapter 6 Summary – Power Moves:

武 Removing the traditional concepts of winning and losing allows the possibility of a win-win resolution.

武 Step aside from the power line of attacking energy.

武 When engaging multiple attackers simultaneously, you should divide your enemies and set them into conflict with each other.

武 Then engage, blend, and guide the energy to your own desired conclusion.

武 Be metaphorically spherical at all times.

Chapter 6 Summary – Pressure Points:

武 It is not only what you say, but it is also the way that you say it that counts.

武 Good timing is a key factor in the successful outcome of any engagement.

武 Choose your ground and timing wisely for any engagement.

武 Visualise tactical interactions and the use of your Chi Energy flow.

Chapter 7: Crisis Media Management

Bad news makes headlines; it is just a fact of modern life. Journalists and TV News networks always want to boost ratings, and it is just another fact that bad news will boost their ratings more easily than good news. Bad news will also travel faster and go further. If something has gone seriously wrong and a crisis has developed for you or your organisation, journalists and TV news networks may make you and your crisis their news headlines!

> *"A lie gets halfway around the world before the truth has a chance to get its pants on".*
>
> Sir Winston Churchill

With respect to Winston Churchill's above quote, rumours tend to spread just as quickly and widely as lies. They also tend to become mutated and distorted in the process, and on social media.

When unexpected negative incidents happen to an individual who already has some media presence or celebrity status, such as an education leader, a corporate executive, or an institution, there will be little or no time to prepare an appropriate and well-thought-out response. The media 'swarm' will descend as fast as they can to be the first to get a breaking news story. If you are the media target, when a crisis occurs and corners you face-to-face, the TV and news media will immediately barrage you with awkward and demanding questions. More importantly, many of these uncomfortable questions could easily catch you off guard. A misspoken word taken out of context by the media could easily present you and your organisation in a highly negative light.

Perception is Reality

How you respond to the media in a crisis is usually critical to your career's survival and general reputation. Will you and your organisation appear competent, caring, and professional? Or will the TV News Media make you and your organisation appear incompetent, foolish, and unprofessional?

Organisations are increasingly faced with handling unexpected crisis issues and politically sensitive situations. At a time of crisis, most leaders usually find themselves and their organisation totally unprepared to manage the media effectively in a hostile crisis. Many people sound foolish and look like the proverbial startled deer in the headlights of an oncoming truck because they have never received professional media training. Pause for a second and imagine how you would feel if the media were attacking you right now and you were being made to appear to be both foolish and incompetent on TV screens all over the country.

Once the TV news media have savaged you and made you appear to be foolish in front of an audience of potentially millions, the next problem you have is keeping your job. It is not uncommon that after someone has been made to appear foolish and incompetent because of a crisis, they've either been forced to quit their job or have been fired. Furthermore, they could have probably avoided the embarrassment if they had prepared in advance by being trained in media crisis management. It is your choice of how you wish to be perceived and what risks you want to take by not safeguarding your job and career. If you value your job, career, lifestyle, and family's reputation, then advanced preparation will be essential to your success in handling the media.

"The tomorrow you envision will never become a reality unless you start making it happen today."

Brian Sterling-Vete

Advanced Preparation is Essential

After performing a friendly news interview with the superintendent of a major Midwestern metropolitan school district in the United States, they shared one of their deep concerns with me. They told me that with a teaching staff of circa 6,000 people and based upon an average statistic of 1 in 10 people being a sex offender, they could unknowingly be employing as many as 600 sex offenders. They told me they considered this situation a time bomb just waiting to explode.

Fact: A crisis almost always strikes without any warning.

Question: *"If a crisis strikes you or your organisation today, are you properly prepared to face the full force of a hostile media with less than 30 minutes' warning?"*

If your answer to the above is no, you are not adequately prepared, and these are the inconvenient facts:

- You do not really care about your personal or professional reputation.
- You do not really care about your job.
- You do not really care if the media make you appear stupid in front of a potentially global audience.
- You do not really care about your family and the fallout which will affect them.
- You do not really care about your lifestyle because you might not even have a job after the crisis is over, since you could very easily be fired.
- You are a gambler, playing for seriously high stakes. These stakes are your job, your family's happiness, and your reputation.

Adopting the 'it will never happen to me' mindset can be detrimental. When a crisis does strike, you may find yourself unprepared and without sympathy from others. This is a missed opportunity for career advancement.

To avoid this, it's crucial for every career-driven individual to take the following points seriously. Here are some tips to help you and your organisation prepare in advance for a potential media crisis.

Stop Procrastinating

Don't fall into the trap of thinking, *'It's a good idea; I'll get around to it soon.'* This passive approach rarely leads to action. The Latin phrase **'Si Vis Pacem, Para Bellum'** is etched into the Royal Navy headquarters in Portsmouth, England, a testament to their commitment to proactive preparation. This phrase applies to you and your organisation as well: **'If you want peace, prepare for war.'**

Have a Plan and Prepare in Advance

It is surprising how many large organisations are ill-prepared to handle a crisis effectively, simply because they do not even have a plan. If you do not have a plan prepared in advance, then the media will metaphorically 'eat you alive.' Your objective in a crisis should always be to end your media engagement with minimum collateral damage and, if possible, to gain a positive media advantage in some way.

I recommend treating your advanced preparation for this similarly to how you would treat a military campaign. Furthermore, when a crisis strikes, you should expect the plan to change, so you need it to be adaptive and evolve.

It's essential to have a plan that allows you to communicate with news media organisations, even those not physically present during your initial interviews and statement releases. Neglecting social media could be a grave mistake, as it's the breeding ground for most rumours, speculations, and allegations. A comprehensive crisis management plan should include strategies for social media engagement.

Social media has enormous power to influence public opinion, and a story can go viral across the globe within an hour. Therefore, have a team of people who are trained and ready to deal specifically with this.

Since it is critically important to begin dealing with a crisis before the crisis happens, here is a checklist of tips and topics which will help you prepare your emergency customised crisis plan:

- Identify all the potential types of crises that could impact you. Once you have done that, then place them in an order of impact importance. This list could include anything from a terrorist attack on your organisation to employee relations.
- Improve your system of monitoring what is happening within and around your organisation. By improving your intelligence gathering and monitoring who is saying/doing what, etc., you will have an advanced warning about any potential threats.
- Create a crisis communications team and ensure that everyone on that team has been fully trained. Your team should comprise representatives from all relevant departments, and each has a deputy to cover them if the lead person is not physically present when a crisis strikes.
- Assign which of your team members will be allowed to speak with the news media and ensure that they receive any additional professional training that may be required.
Remember, these people will be a primary source of relevant information. Journalists want an easy life, so if they can get the relevant facts they need from you or your key people promptly, then they will have much less incentive to look for alternative and potentially more damaging sources.
- Develop and assign a command structure to your crisis team. This should be a critical path procedure that activates when a crisis strikes. As the crisis increases in importance, so does the communication about it. It should progress logically up the chain of command until the top person has been summoned to deal with the most serious of crises. Always keep the command chain informed about a crisis that has been identified, but you should only escalate the severity of the situation when necessary.
- Remember that lawyers do not always handle a crisis well because they usually approach issues from the perspective of minimising legal exposure. This is not always the best way to

handle a media crisis that could severely destroy or damage your public reputation.

- Respond to a crisis in a timely fashion, and do not allow rumours any time to begin and develop. Remember, the media will always want a statement, so it is a good idea to prepare some generic holding statements in advance.

  Even if you simply state that you are aware that a serious incident has occurred or that a problem has arisen, this will relieve some pressure and buy you some time to think before you need to make a more detailed statement.

- Use your private label and secure video distribution portal to prepare generic video messages in advance about a crisis that has developed. Private label portals such as Eduvision allow global distribution of secure video content, complete with any attached files you may want to support the statement with. If you do not already have one deployed, then get one ASAP, and have certain private channels configured which are only for use in the event of a crisis.

- If you do not already have a Facebook page and/or Twitter account, then get one fast.

- Devise and implement a social media policy as a guide to empower the use of social media channels responsibly in a way that builds the organisation's image. It will help you enormously by doing this well in advance of a crisis occurring.

- Implement a training program and devise rules/guidelines for anyone representing your organisation on social media. Appoint a social media manager and account administrator/s. The manager should securely hold all passwords.

- Devise and deploy a social media management system that allows monitoring, publishing, and conversion tracking. A good monitoring system can help you monitor what is being said about your organisation, and more importantly, it will alert you to potential issues *before* they become a problem.

With all the above in place, ensure all your relevant facts and figures are complete, accurate, and properly collated. If you do not, it will appear that you are either trying to hide something or that you are incompetent. Either way, it is not good.

Once you have prepared all the data you will need in advance, you will need to keep it updated regularly once the system is deployed. This should include general data sheets, maps, and advanced data sheets specifically for law enforcement and fire departments. These should also include building schematics that will help enormously in the event of a hostage, gunman, fire, or similar crisis.

Ensure that your media headquarters and communication rooms can handle multiple types and levels of communication. They should have reliable internet with high bandwidth, printing capability, computers, stationery, good lighting, desk space, etc.

Rehearsing mock scenarios in advance with your team will help you iron out any unforeseen problems in your planning. It would be best if you decided in advance which members of your team from each department will be allowed to meet the media. Everyone chosen to be the primary media contact in each department should rehearse mock high-pressure media interviews. They should be ruthlessly questioned and cross-questioned in the training scenarios and under the scrutiny of the rest of the team. This will help identify those team members who will crack under pressure, so you can reassign their roles in advance of a crisis.

As the British Special Air Service Regiment believe:
'Train hard - fight easy.'

Prepare for the Media Scrum

When the media finally arrive, it may feel like you have suddenly been placed in the centre of a Rugby scrum. It is worth searching for video examples of this online, and you will see precisely what I mean because it is brutal! It is essential to be well-rehearsed and confident enough to face a live audience if necessary. It is also worth practising your public speaking skills regularly. This will help you appear more professional and polished when you speak to a live audience. Being confident, professional, and polished in your presentation skills will take some of the pressure off you, allowing you to focus more of your attention on taking control of the media engagement.

Choose Your Ground

It is always better to choose where and when to engage the media rather than have the media choose it for you. By maintaining control of this critical point, you will maintain better overall control of the situation. It is worth remembering that TV news crews will always want something visual to show, and they might even want to show something dramatic if it is relevant to the story. This makes it even more critical to maintain control of all the used locations.

Video

Video is an extremely powerful medium that is almost obligatory in today's media and news environment. Furthermore, a video is far superior to a written statement in delivering a powerful message. Poorly conceived, composed, and written statements can often make you appear guilty, even if you are not.

Public media platforms, such as YouTube, are not a serious option for any organisation that wishes to maintain privacy or security. Since they are basically public domain, it is quite challenging to manage media content effectively once video clips are uploaded. Therefore, you should always use a secure private-label TV and video distribution system.

Public video portals such as YouTube or Vimeo are only helpful if you want a message to become part of the public domain and viral as part of your overall media strategy. They are no good for anything except getting you into trouble. If you are an educator and you allow your students to use YouTube, they are potentially only one or two clicks away from pornography. This means you are potentially only one or two clicks away from a media crisis that may cost you your job. Public domain platforms such as YouTube and Vimeo could be part of the reason you have a crisis in the first place.

I recommend JDL's Eduvision platform because it is easy to use and secure. You can create multiple channels, perform live broadcast streaming, and attach documents to videos. It has the same robust network backbone that many TV broadcasters use.

The Eduvision platform was originally designed as a secure system for schools to help keep students safe; however, it works equally well in the corporate world. More importantly, it provides multiple secure private TV channels to get your targeted messages out to the world, and you can host as many media-holding statements as needed.

This system will help buy you precious thinking time before the TV news crews finally arrive and want to record a video interview. The Eduvision system also allows you to update your messages in almost real-time because it integrates with TechSmith's Fuse software.

This integration lets you record personal, news-style video statements via your cell phone or tablet and immediately upload them to your pre-prepared EduVision channels. These channels and your video broadcasts can then be directed securely to whomever you wish. It even allows you to time the delivery of your broadcasts or only make them available between certain times and dates. You can also set the system so each video is only available for viewing, downloading, or both.

Silence is Golden - Except in a Crisis

No matter the situation, even if it is dire, it is always best to provide a steady flow of information to the news media. It is never wise to clam up and pretend that a crisis has not happened or does not exist.

The longer you leave the media without proper, detailed, and accurate information, the sooner they will draw their own conclusions. Once that process has started, and even if they only have limited information, they will make up an interim report for themselves.

This is always much more damaging than even the direst information you could supply them with. By seeming to avoid the media, the public will perceive you as guilty, foolish, incompetent, or having something to hide.

This will leave you with an even bigger credibility deficit than before, which you must then try to recover when you eventually meet the media in person. Do not allow the media to speculate about what happened and exaggerate the story just because you chose to pretend it was not happening and remained silent.

It is important to remember that, in general, organisations that delay or even refuse to communicate with journalists often suffer more hostile and damning news coverage as a result.

Think Fast, But Talk Slowly

During an intense media engagement, you must embrace and engage all your Mental Martial Arts strategies and tactics. You must be polished in making the correct word choice, biasing, engaging, body language, verbal somatotyping, directing conversation flow, redirecting attacking questions, etc., since you will need to be good at all these things, practice, practice, and practice in advance.

Do not allow yourself to be derailed by persistent journalists who will try to prevent you from conveying the message you want to deliver. If necessary, use the Falklands Technique, which was made famous by British Prime Minister Margaret Thatcher during the Falklands War with Argentina.

The media converged outside 10 Downing Street in London, where a statement would be made at a specific time. It was about the first military action of the war when the S.A.S. and Royal Marines Commandos retook the first of the Falkland Islands, which Argentina invaded in 1982.

John Nott, the Secretary of Defence at the time, made a carefully crafted statement of fact about this to the media. However, the media demanded more information, and once the statement had been delivered, journalists proceeded to bombard Mr Nott from all angles with seriously challenging questions.

Then, Prime Minister Thatcher intervened and took complete control of the media engagement. She did not allow herself to be derailed for a second. She used word power, commanding vocals, and body language to silence the press pack. She skilfully redirected their hostile energy by telling them clearly and concisely that they should be satisfied with the good news.

I have documented the complete engagement below because it is a superb example of how to control a frenzied media pack during a crisis. It is well worth watching the video on the internet. The transcript below is from when the defence secretary met with the national and world media outside 10 Downing Street in London, the home of the British Prime Minister. He gave an official statement about the first action of the war.

John Nott to the media

"The message we have got is that British troops landed on South Georgia this afternoon, shortly after 4 pm London time.

They have now successfully taken control of Grytviken; at about 6 pm London time, the white flag was hoisted in Grytviken beside the Argentine flag.

Shortly afterwards, the Argentine forces there surrendered to British forces.

The Argentine forces offered only limited resistance to the British troops.

Our forces were landed by helicopter and were supported by several warships, together with a Royal Fleet Auxiliary.

During the first phase of this opinion, our own helicopters engaged the Argentine submarine, Santa Fé, off South Georgia.

This submarine was detected at first light and was engaged because it posed a threat to our men and to the British warships launching the landing.

So far, no British casualties have been reported.

At present, we have no information on the Argentine casualty position.

The Commander of the operation has sent the following message: "Be pleased to inform Her Majesty that the White Ensign flies alongside the Union Jack in South Georgia. God save the Queen."

Media Questions:

What happens next, Mr Nott? What's your reaction …?

John Nott (He did not react; he said nothing more and let Prime Minister Thatcher take over.)

Margaret Thatcher (answering emphatically before turning towards the door of Number 10 Downing Street).

"Just rejoice at that news and congratulate our forces and the Marines."

"Goodnight."

(Margaret Thatcher then begins walking to the door.)

Media Questions

"Are we going to war with Argentina, Mrs Thatcher?"

Margaret Thatcher (pauses on the doorstep and ignores the question to deliver only the message she wants to convey)

'Rejoice."

(No more information was given, and Margaret Thatcher and John Nott both re-entered Number 10 Downing Street.)

Around the World, Around the Clock

If the above scenario sounds challenging, then I make no apologies for pointing out that your role in any media crisis is crucial. Since a crisis can happen at any time and without any warning, your preparedness 24 hours a day, 7 days a week, and 365 days per year is essential.

You need to be able to fully deploy your crisis team and begin implementing the plan from the moment a crisis strikes. Even if you do not, the global news machine and social media operate on a 24/7 schedule. This is the hard reality you are faced with, and these are just some of the challenges you and your organisation might be facing today.

Special Tips for Schools and Educational Leadership

Education leadership should prepare education-specific fact packs. These packs should be continually updated as needed so that they are always current and vital information is ready for immediate distribution in a crisis. One pack should provide an overview of the entire district, and additional packs should be specific to each school building, administrative building, or general campus area within the district's purview. These packs should comprise fact sheets, site maps, a contact sheet, and printed statements about the specific crisis event.

In addition to these, you need to prepare advanced data packs, which are much more detailed than the media packs. These are specifically for use by law enforcement officers and fire rescue teams. They should contain additional information, which might include non-standard potential entrance and egress points to the buildings, power supply data, where chemicals and other hazardous substances are stored, communication wiring, security camera network schematics, etc.

It is not just a good idea but a necessity to meet in advance with your law enforcement, fire department, local government, and even military departments. This collaborative effort ensures that all eventualities are covered and valuable insights are shared. This level of detailed, advanced planning will help enormously in the event of a crisis in a school or on campus.

Collate details about all team members and how they can be contacted in a crisis. Deploy video systems such as Panasonic's Studio in a Box. This is essentially a mobile mini-TV studio that can help you create your news statement videos.

Then, if you have deployed them in advance, EduVision by JDL Horizons will handle the dissemination of your secure video communications, TechSmith's Fuse software will handle your real-time video updates, and School Messenger will help you handle mass school-parent communications via text, and email etc.

Having all of this in place and operational in advance makes handling an incredibly stressful situation a whole lot less stressful than it might otherwise be. You also need to identify and assign certain areas which you will use for the following:

- Video broadcast room. If you already have one, it will usually be your school TV news desk room. If you do not have one, create one.
- Media control headquarters. In a crisis, this will be where all communications flow into and out of your organisation.

Take a tip from Hollywood and rehearse, rehearse, and then rehearse again. Plan and perform emergency preparedness exercises that closely resemble serious real-life crises. This will help you identify and then iron out any logistical issues and flaws in your overall plan. It will also give board members, faculty members, students, and parents confidence in your leadership.

When journalists interview you, it is nothing more than a basic energy exchange. However, in a crisis, the energy directed at you by the journalist will be intense, possibly hostile, and almost certainly attack you and your organisation in some way.

Traditionally, the bigger and more powerful opponent will almost always gain the advantage in a direct, back-and-forth linear energy exchange. In this case, it would be the journalist and the TV network.

Therefore, always use the strategies and tactics of Mental Martial Arts. Do not express a solid metaphoric shape, which will make it challenging for you to move out of the attacking energy line. If you do, you will usually end up trading linear toe-to-toe exchanges and usually be on the defensive.

Instead, remain fluid and flexible, making it hard for your opponent to corner you in an attack. If they do, then expect them to drill you down on a specific point, which could be a problem. Always engage the journalist in the same way as you would engage an opponent in physical martial arts. Engage them and then redirect their message and any implications it may carry to your own desired conclusion.

> *"You must be shapeless and formless like water. Water can drip, it can flow, and it can crash. Be like water, my friend."*
> Bruce Lee

Special printable resources are available from the FBI, FEMA, and MI5 about preventing and increasing the chances of surviving terrorist attacks. They contain advice about how to survive a general terrorist shooting attack. Also, how to survive a school shooting.

In the following example scenario, a former sex worker has been found working as an English teacher at a high school. The media have found out and are looking for a juicy headline story. In the first scenario, a single journalist is interviewing the school superintendent. In the diagrams, the journalist is represented as an explosion of energy, and the superintendent is represented as a sphere.

Journalist: "Allowing a sex worker to work as a teacher must mean that your screening processes are flawed?"

Superintendent: *"That's a good question. Let me help clarify your facts. A former sex worker deliberately hid critical information about her past to become a member of the faculty. As you know, the screening process we use meets all state standards, and since there are no state records kept of sex workers, we appreciate your help in alerting other schools to the possibility of the same thing happening to them."*

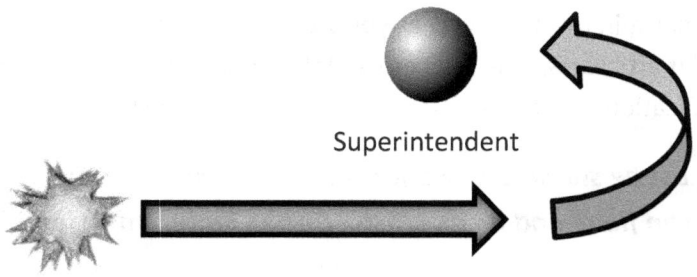

Superintendent

Journalist   Attacking energy line

(The superintendent metaphorically steps sideways, out of the journalist's direct attacking energy line. At the same time, the superintendent begins to blend their energy while maintaining constant engagement with the journalist to begin redirecting the attack.)

Journalist: *"Aren't your screening processes flawed? Surely there's a better system?"*

Superintendent: *"Our screening processes are laid down by the state, and you're right in that the state needs to* *review the system. We really appreciate you helping here."*

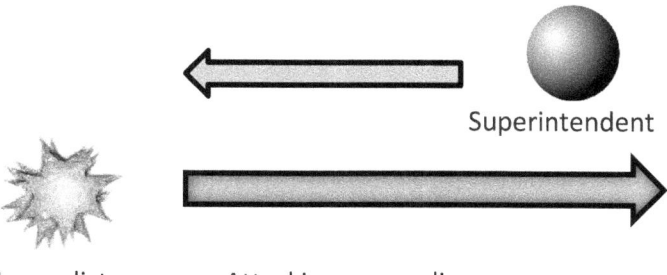

Journalist   Attacking energy line.

(The superintendent slipped past the attacking question and began moving toward the journalist's perspective to better align their energy and objectives. At the same time, they continue to maintain their engagement with the journalist. The superintendent also redirects the energy to begin an attack on the faceless "State." In doing so, they allude to some implied 'help' that the journalist is giving the public by reporting this matter.)

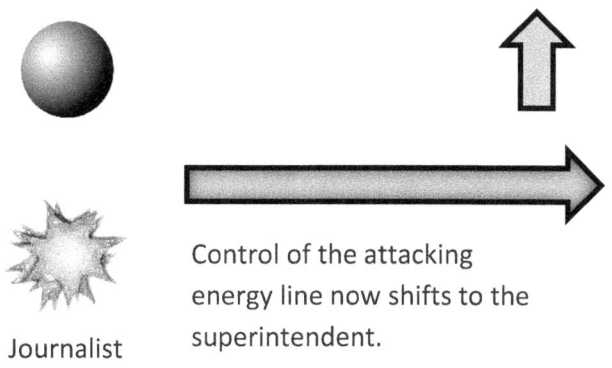

Journalist   Control of the attacking energy line now shifts to the superintendent.

(The attacking energy line of the journalist has been dissipated. The superintendent has appealed to their ego and drawn the journalists into believing that they are helping to get state laws modified for the benefit of everyone. The use of keywords and phrases is vital. These will create

and maintain a low level of confusion in the minds of the journalists. Suggesting, or alluding to, some vague agreement to help and to be of public service due to being like-minded can be a powerful weapon.)

Journalist:	*"Weren't your students exposed to danger from this woman?"*
Superintendent:	*"Thanks for helping me clear this up. People need to know the facts, and these are that our students were only exposed to the risk of learning significantly more about the English language. This is because the woman in question was the most highly qualified and the best English teacher that we've ever had."*
Journalist:	*"Since the students were exposed to a person who was a former sex worker, weren't you afraid that she'd possibly use her body to solicit sex again with some students?*
Superintendent:	*"Good point, and you're right that anyone could be working with a former sex worker or someone with a hidden past. As we established earlier, there's no official register of former sex workers, so literally anyone could have once been one, and no one would know. Even the person you're working next to right now here at work.*

(The superintendent gestures toward the camera crew.) We agree. It's a real problem that the state needs to address. We all appreciate your help here. Thank *you."*

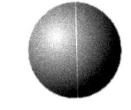

Superintendent

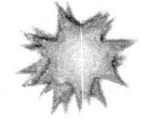

Journalist

Aligned energy line.

The attacking energy line is now diffusing into nothing, and both parties have a basic, commonly aligned energy perspective, just as if the engagement had never happened. The strategy and tactics used here will even work if you find yourself at an extreme disadvantage or face several journalists at once.

The key is to remain calm, remember your training, and always engage your opponent with a relaxed and highly focused mind. In the following scenario, the challenge intensifies as the superintendent must confront not one but two aggressive journalists simultaneously. This situation underscores the necessity of the strategies and tactics outlined in this guide.

The great Martial Arts Master Morihei Ueshiba once said:

"One should be prepared to receive 99% of an enemy's attack and stare death in the face to illuminate the path to victory."

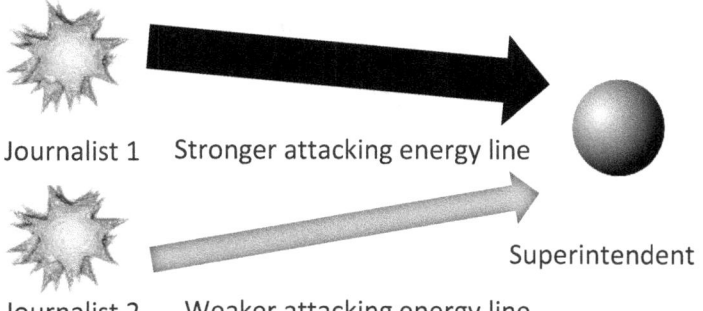

The attacking energy lines from both journalists simultaneously attack the superintendent. The black arrow represents the stronger of the two attacks, and the grey arrow represents the weaker of the two.

Journalist 1: "How could a sex worker be allowed to work at your school as a teacher?"

Journalist 2: "Surely your screening processes are flawed?"

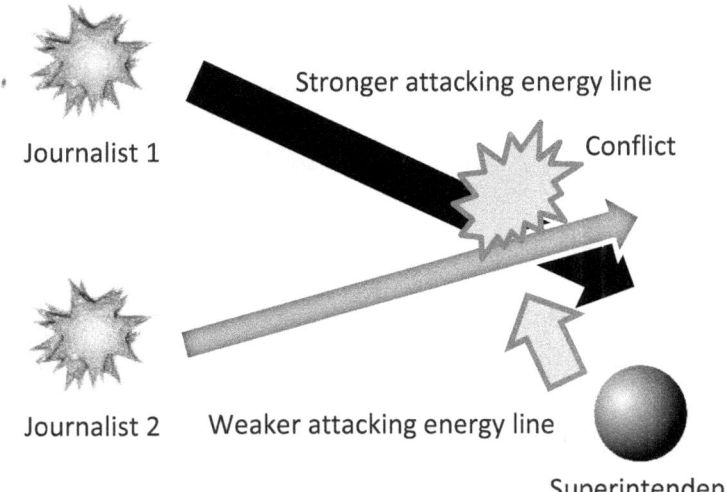

Superintendent: (Looking directly at Journalist 1 while at the same time deliberately ignoring Journalist 2)

> "That's a good question, thank you. Let me help you clarify your facts. A former sex worker deliberately hid important information about her past to become a member of the faculty."

Superintendent: (Looking directly at Journalist 2)

> "As journalist 1 mentioned earlier at the briefing...

(There is always confusion in crisis journalism, and no one really knows 'who said what' in the press scrum or briefing sessions.
However, this strategy is useful because it helps to cause conflict and confusion among journalists.
This is because they all want to deliver the key questions and believe they know all the facts.)

> ...the screening process we use meets all state standards, and since there are no state records kept of sex workers, we appreciate your help in alerting other schools to the possibility of the same thing happening to them."

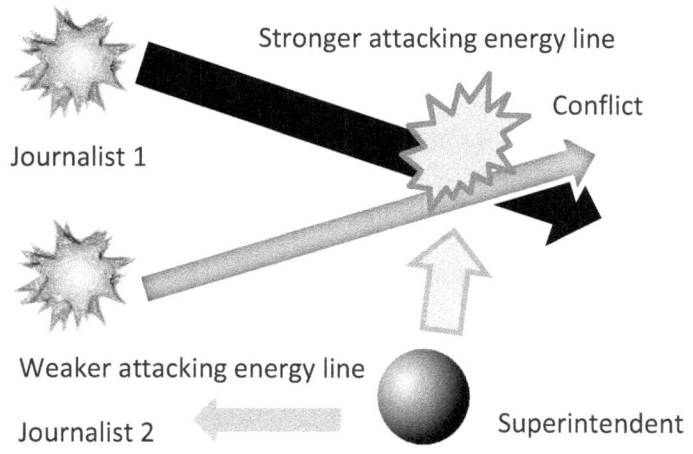

Journalist 1: *"Aren't your screening processes flawed? Surely there's a better system?"*

Superintendent: (To Journalist 1)
"Our screening processes are laid down by the state, and YOU'RE right, in that the state needs to review the system. We appreciate you helping here."

(The superintendent now concentrates their attack against the strongest journalist. At the same time, he/she will seek to create more confusion and conflict between them.)

Journalist 2: *"Surely there's a better system?"*

Superintendent: (To Journalist 2)
"Thanks for supporting us in this matter. You're right; the state should look at how to improve the system. As you recall, I believe someone from Journalist 1's network was looking at exactly this not long ago."

Journalist 1: *"Weren't your students exposed to danger from this woman?"*

Superintendent: (To Journalist 1)

"It's good to know that our students were only exposed to the risk of learning significantly more about the English language. Despite the woman in question being a former sex worker, she was the most highly qualified and the best English teacher that we have ever had. Thanks for highlighting this."

(Journalist 1 is now slightly confused and is being increasingly led to believe that they have taken some credit for helping to highlight an important issue.)

Journalist 2: "Your students were exposed to a person who was a former sex worker."

Superintendent: (To Journalist 2)

"Thank you for helping me clear this up in your last question."

(Journalist 2 is now becoming increasingly confused)

Journalist 2: "Weren't you afraid that she'd use her body to solicit sex again with the older students?"

Superintendent: (Addressing both Journalists)

"Thanks for helping to clarify this. You're both right that anyone could be working with a former sex worker or someone with a hidden past. As we've already established earlier, there are no official records kept of former sex workers, so anyone could have been one. Even the person you're working next to right now, here at work.

(The superintendent gestures towards the camera crew and to the weaker of the two journalists.)

We agree. It's a real problem that the state needs to address. We all appreciate both of you helping here; it makes a real difference. Thank you."

(This technique continues to destabilise the combined attack of both journalists. At the same time, the superintendent continues to move towards blending and aligning the official position with that of Journalist 1. He/she also sets Journalist 2, with the weaker of the two questions, into slight conflict with Journalist 1.)

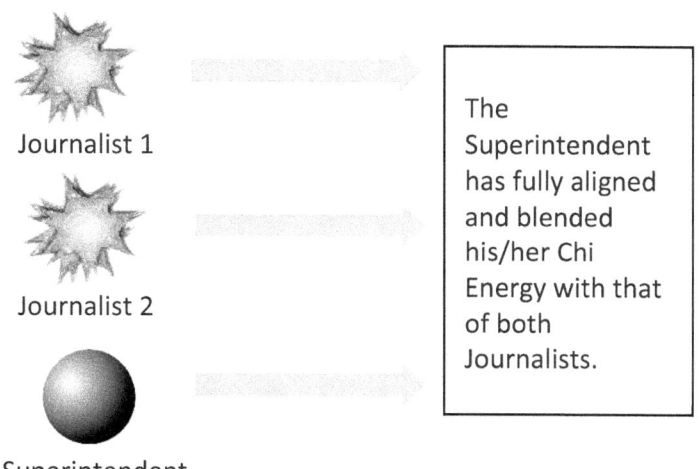

"You cannot buy insurance after the crisis event. Similarly, you cannot prepare to face the media once they are on your doorstep and demanding to see you."

Brian Sterling-Vete

Tips to Help When Appearing on TV and Video

It is now almost certain that you will be required to appear in front of the camera at some point during your business or social life. To help you with this, here are a few tips that will help to make the process much more enjoyable and rewarding. They will also help you express yourself to the world in a better, more polished, and professional way.

It is important to remember that a camera will pick up even the slightest movement, especially when it is in close-up framing, so do not use excessive and over-the-top gestures. Stage actors understand this technique very well. It is also why they use what might seem to be over-emphasised dramatic gestures when rehearsing or performing on stage. Since the audience in a theatre is always some distance away and certainly not as close as an interview camera, they need to use more exaggerated gestures to make it appear 'right' to the audience.

As you gain more experience in front of the camera, you'll start to appreciate the power of mastering certain basic techniques. These techniques will not only enhance your on-screen image but also empower you to express yourself confidently and professionally.

Flexibility is key when it comes to different camera shots. Always inquire about the framing of the shot during an interview. This information will guide you on the level of expressiveness required. Whether it's a wide shot or a close-up, your adaptability will ensure you present yourself in the most effective way.

This is because you will appear smaller on the screen, effectively putting your audience at a greater viewing distance from you, just like an actor on stage.

Conversely, in a close-up shot, you must slightly tone down your expressions and any expressive behaviour. If you do not, you will appear exaggerated, 'hammy' and unconvincing. Therefore, if you are appearing on camera and you are asked to:

- 武 Turn a shoulder in or out of frame.
- 武 Step a little to the left or the right.
- 武 Move your head slightly.
- 武 Look one way or the other.
- 武 Adjust your eye line.

Always start by asking about the frame size being used for the shot, and then adjust your position accordingly with the appropriate scale of movement. As a rule, do not make any huge adjustments and movements because you are probably already quite close to the desired position the camera requires.

Some people who are nervous about being on camera may express excessive displacement signals, such as shuffling on the spot, tapping with their feet, or having a wandering eyeline. These are not good because they detract from any performance, and there is a high probability that the camera will magnify their movements to the audience.

Be patient with the camera crew and the director. Work with them and help them create the best presentation possible. Do not be unduly worried or nervous if it seems that they are taking a long time to set up the shot. They are simply factoring in many technical options that will help you look great, so help them do that!

If you know in advance that you will appear on camera, I suggest you practice your presentation alone in front of a full-length mirror before filming. Even if you do not know what questions you will be asked during the interview, practice reading a passage from a book professionally.

Using this technique, your body language, macro gestures, vocal tone, inflexion, intonation, pitch, and cadence should be carefully planned. It is a highly worthwhile exercise because each time you see the video played back, you will be happy with the image you portray instead of cringing in embarrassment and hoping it will end quickly.

Your overall public image is critical and should be carefully considered. Everyone who appears regularly in the public eye has already done this. During her rise to power, Baroness Margaret Thatcher, the former British Prime Minister, had to carefully study her vocal tone, intonation, and depth of her voice. Media professionals advised her that she would have a more significant on-screen impact when appearing on TV and delivering live audience speeches if she lowered her vocal pitch. This obviously worked exceptionally well.

Sound Bites

When answering a question during an interview, the best replies are usually sound bites because they are the most likely to be used and the easiest to edit. A sound bite is just a short sentence that encapsulates the essence of what you wish to say. It is a summary of the information, which increases the impact of what you say to the listener.

A good sound bite is like a concise elevator speech covering the critical points of all the information you want to convey. It is usually delivered within a 10 to 30-second period. Anything more than that is rambling and confusing to the listener, and it will probably not get used in the final edit. Keep it short and deliver a series of knockout 'punches' in what you say and how you say it.

321, 123, Um, Er, So…

Avoid using filler words like "um" and "er." These will detract from your overall presentation and dramatically reduce the impact of your message. When replying to a question on camera by delivering a sound bite, you should always avoid beginning your delivery with the words "so," "well," or any other kind of lead-in filler word.

In most cases, people have no idea they use these words until they see a video recording of their presentation. Once it is recorded on video, it is too late to do anything about it. If you need to set the intonation of your delivery, then use your inner monologue to say the lead-in words in your head before you deliver the sound bite on video.

Practice using the 321 - 123 rules when delivering any kind of video presentation. This allows the editor to cut your clips together more easily, which in turn only makes you look and sound better.

The rule is simple. Before you begin speaking, set your eye-line onto your target, and then, when the cue is given, use your inner monologue to silently count down 3, 2, 1 in your head before speaking. At the end of your delivery, maintain your eye-line on your target and then silently count 1, 2, 3 in your head. This technique gives you editing lead-in and lead-out time, which the media teams will love.

Furthermore, it will make you extremely popular with journalists and TV crews, so you will become their interview subject of choice when they need a thought leader statement from an educator.

Characterisation and Polished Presentation.

If you are concerned about your performance, confidence, and overall appearance during live presentations and on-screen TV interviews, characterising them can help you overcome these problems quickly.

Many people are surprised to learn that some well-known actors are often quite shy and reserved in their private lives. Sometimes, they are so shy and reserved that they do not like to make public appearances, and some are even averse to simply appearing as themselves when asked to give a live presentation to a group of fans.

People often have a tough time understanding why this is. They get confused between perception and reality. This is because they are used to seeing the actors playing highly confident heroes and villains on TV and movie screens.

Why are some actors so shy in everyday life yet appear hugely confident when they appear in movies watched by millions of people? The answer is simple. The actors absorb themselves into the role of another character, someone who is not who they really are. In other words, they act. The characters they construct and portray have all the confidence and abilities to do anything they choose, so that the actors can do the same things on the screen.

Many businesspeople who are required to deliver presentations and speeches to large audiences or are required to give TV interviews often use this same technique. They envision themselves as an imaginary character with all the confidence and professionalism that the real person lacks. Therefore, if you are ever nervous or concerned about your presentation on stage or on-screen, then you should try doing the same. An easy way to learn how to do this is by envisioning a character from a movie you know who possesses all the qualities you require to deliver your presentation.

The better you know the movie plot and the character you envision, the easier it will be. Scientists have proven that the human brain does not recognise much difference between the real world and a highly detailed visualisation. Therefore, you can use this technique to your advantage to help create the characterisations you need in your professional life.

A professional actor would draw much information from the script about the background details surrounding the character they must create. Therefore, the more detail you can envision about your imaginary character, the better your overall performance will be.

It is often easier to envision and portray a character from a movie you have already seen and know. Your objective should be to develop a multi-dimensional character with a rich backstory from which you can draw. Imagine this person has become 'you' every time you need to present on stage or when you need to deliver a TV interview. If you use the technique of envisioning a movie character you already know, then the actor you are emulating has done all the work in advance for you. You can use the actor's in-depth characterisation in that role to help you make your presentations with newfound confidence and flair.

Chapter 8: Handling Negative Social Media

Suppose you are ever impacted by something negative in the media. In that case, the lingering effects of being found at or near the top of internet searches can damage you, like lingering radiation poisoning. Even if the story is not big enough for TV news to cover, search engines and social media platforms will always make your negative publicity appear near the top of page 1.

The first thing to remember is that it is challenging to delete negative reviews and articles on the Internet unless you can contact the person who posted them and ask them to remove the bad reviews. Many individuals and small companies will pitch you for a job doing this, but unless there is a genuinely serious problem to deal with, they will only do what I suggest in this section. Therefore, if you have the skillset and time to handle it yourself or appoint someone with similar skills, you probably do not need to employ a subcontractor. However, a professional subcontractor would be best if you are out of your depth, or the subject of the negative media is particularly harmful and extensive.

Do Not Make a Fuss

As a rule, the greater the fuss about you wanting to take any negative posts down, the more the post owners will think that your content is even more valuable than they first thought it was. This will only make it more attractive to them and more challenging and expensive to try to pay them off as you attempt to remove it.

I have also known cases where someone has paid to have something removed, only to find that another similar site pops up with the same content. The same people probably own this new site, but the contract and payment for removing the post only referred to the original site. Then, the whole process must start over again. It is a form of legal blackmail, which is how these unscrupulous people make money.

Remember, this is not slander; it is the internet and full of people who make money out of cyber blackmail and your negative press. Therefore, you should always approach it from the perspective that the perpetrators of the negativity will not willingly delete the negative posts. Therefore, an excellent way to get rid of bad reviews is to bury them.

Bury the Posts

The best way to get rid of negative postings is to bury them deeper and deeper down the pages of search engines. Do not stop posting until they're past pages 4 or 5 on all major search engines. Before trying to bury any harmful online content, it is always best to note why they've ranked on the first page and what keywords you want to use to help you bury them.

Based on the answer to these questions, you will then determine how much time, work, and money it might take to bury them deep enough so they pose only a minimal threat. The bonus is that the more positive posts you make, the more you will boost your internet image and your ability to be easily found in search engines. Make notes of the following

- The authority, age, and quality of the website that is posting the content.
- How relevant the content is written is related to the keyword used in the search.
- The number and quality of sites linking back to the original site hosting the article.

These points are also the primary reasons why most sites show at the top of the search results for any given name or phrase. Remember this to implement these same practices on your websites and manage your general online reputation.

Consider setting up a WordPress Blog to complement your websites and personal brands. This straightforward process, especially for those with a basic understanding of web-related matters, can yield significant results. By consistently posting valuable content, you can attract others to link their sites to yours, thereby enhancing your site's authority and page rankings.

Don't underestimate the power of creating profiles on major social media networks. This free and straightforward process can significantly boost your online visibility. Platforms like Twitter, Facebook, LinkedIn, YouTube, Pinterest, and Instagram are highly ranked by Google, making them ideal for improving your search results. Remember to create both personal and professional profiles and websites. Here is an approximate breakdown of each social media platform's (current at the time of writing) Domain Authority (DA), with the higher score being better than the lower scores. (correct at the time of writing)

- Twitter: DA 100
- Facebook: DA 100
- YouTube: DA 100
- Vimeo: DA 98
- Instagram: DA 97
- Yelp: DA 94
- PR.com: DA 78

Since these sites are ranked highly by all the leading search engines, they are particularly important. Also, Google has a great deal of trust in them, especially on sites they already own, such as YouTube. These sites are so good that even if they are blasted with bad links, they serve as a form of spam filter if the DA is high enough. For example, at the time of writing, Facebook had over 15,000,0000,0000 links, allowing you to build backlinks to your Facebook page without fear of being reprimanded. Also, since Google owns YouTube, it is another excellent reason why using video is so important. When picking the properties to rank, be sure to look for these attributes:

- Properties with Verified High Domain Authority.
- Properties that shed a positive light on you and your organisation's image.

- Properties that allow you to link directly to yourself and your organisation's associated websites.
- Properties that have you and your organisation in the URL or tag.
- Properties with positive reviews from customers, such as Foursquare and Google+, etc.

Do Not Forget to Blog

In addition to the above, additional blogs can be built on other free content platforms that are rising in profile. Some of these lesser-known free blog hosting services rank quite well in search results, so do not neglect them. They work much like the leading social media sites that rank well, and free blog services like BlogSpot and WordPress achieve the same results. It is important to blog and post only quality content and some links back to it. The easiest way to get quality content is to scour the internet several pages down each search and then republish the better blogs under your different blog profiles. This is always much easier than writing them yourself.

Recognising that content is 'King', and there's a perpetual need for more, inviting reputable guest writers to contribute content in exchange for promotion and a link back from their site is beneficial. This approach not only brings fresh perspectives but also aids in building quality links back to your websites. It's a win-win situation that can elevate your personal and public profiles with free exposure to new audiences.

Be Aggressive

Merely creating social media and blog accounts and posting content once or twice is not enough. Active management is crucial. Content needs to be sourced, prepared, and scheduled for posting twice a day, every day. This helps maintain the high value of your social media platforms and ensures a consistent posting strategy. If someone comments about one of your negative online media articles, it may cause it to rise in the search engines temporarily. However, maintaining or even increasing your consistent posting strategy will eventually bury the negative online media posts deeper and deeper in the search engines, reducing their threat to a minimum.

Use Infographics

Everyone likes a good infographic, which can easily be created through sites like Piktochart or Infogram. Infographics, or Information graphics to use the full unabbreviated name, are graphic visual representations of information, data or knowledge intended to present information quickly and clearly. One of the main reasons why infographics work so well is that people love to share them and might end up back at your site in the process. This means that it will increase link/traffic back to the places where you need it most, which results in higher-placed search rankings.

Use Strategic Media/Press Releases

Many press releases will still get picked up and indexed by search engines. However, the releases must always be strategic in nature and deployment. This means that we only prepare releases to support positive and well-thought-out campaigns. Do not fall into the trap of churning out media releases every week because they will soon have little or no impact. In fact, news agencies will soon begin to see you as a supplier of rubbish merely to gain free publicity.

Many news releases go wrong because they are not relevant to 99% of the people using the internet, so you should always be on the lookout for whatever might be the next trend. Riding the crest of a current trend will have an enormously positive effect on helping you bury your negative media in search engines.

Chapter 9:
Confidence, Character Flaws, and 'Stuff'

Confidence and courage usually go hand in hand. Furthermore, it is often as simple as doing the right thing at the right time, demonstrating both qualities. However, this is typically easy to say yet extremely hard to do. I will briefly examine some defining factors in building a healthy personal attitude, good self-esteem, and confidence without arrogance.

Confidence, or self-confidence, could be described as being certain that something you envision or predict is correct. Therefore, it is important to be sure that your chosen course of action is also correct. Another possible definition of the term 'confidence' is having subjective and optimistic certainty that you are correct in your thoughts, a course of action, and your expectation of overall success.

Therefore, self-confidence is perhaps all of the above, plus an absolute belief in yourself to know your true capabilities. It follows then that to be over-confident would be to have an unrealistic belief in yourself and your abilities. One of the great difficulties in quantifying and defining confidence is that it is a subjective quality. It is only proven to be correct after the fact. Perhaps confidence could even be described as a self-fulfilling prophecy. You may succeed at something only because you have confidence, ability, or both. Therefore, a person typically defined as self-confident is usually quiet, calm, charismatic, independent, and exudes presence and optimism.

A good way to observe confidence portrayed in others is to watch movie actors portray confident people. Choose a movie where a hero faces a daunting task and note how they resolve the situation. Most movie heroes are charismatic and always confident in their chosen course of action. They also usually inspire and instil confidence in other characters in the movie as they work to succeed through adversity. You can also observe the lack of confidence being portrayed similarly by others.

Positive Mental Attitude

The concept of a Positive Mental Attitude, or PMA, was first developed by Napoleon Hill in his book Think and Grow Rich. Later, Napoleon Hill and W. Clement Stone wrote Success Through a Positive Mental Attitude. This book defines PMA as possessing the right mental attitude comprised of characteristics symbolised by such words as faith, integrity, hope, optimism, courage, initiative, generosity, tolerance, tact, kindliness, and good common sense.

PMA is linked to your self-talk and has been proven to enhance overall performance, ability, and confidence. However, I believe that there are two kinds of PMA. The first is superficial PMA, where a person is confident and positively focused only while things are going well. Since their PMA is superficial and not integral to their core, their PMA erodes quickly and eventually disappears when things get tough. They have no resilience to deal with the real hardships of life, and they crumble. As they do so, they reveal their core nature, which is weak and ineffectual, like a proverbial 'paper tiger.'

The second kind of PMA is what I call Core PMA, which is entirely different. A person with Core PMA will remain realistically optimistic no matter what happens around them. Their life may be stricken with the worst kind of personal illness, family illness, or forces beyond anyone's control that might cause their business to collapse, and yet their core PMA remains constant. They always stay positive, focused, kind, loving, generous, and realistic. I am proud to know my trusted friend and visionary business partner, Simon Earle, who endured all the above and more, and yet he always remained optimistic.

Another man with true Core PMA, whom I am proud to know personally, is Sam Rafowitz. I first met Sam when I performed a TV interview with him, which was to be included in Steven Spielberg's

Holocaust Memorial Archive. Before I met Sam, his son Ivan had warned me that his father was a true force of nature, and he was right! Sam has Core PMA in a way that few others could ever even dream about having. He is a shining example of how staying positive at your core can sustain you despite enduring suffering and challenges beyond all imagination.

Sam was a young man when Hitler invaded Poland, triggering the start of World War 2. Unfortunately, the vile Nazi invaders soon rounded up Sam, his mother, and the rest of his family, together with many other completely innocent people. Why? Simply because they were Jewish. He was first interned in a hard labour camp and then eventually in several concentration camps.

During World War 2, Sam had the questionable 'privilege' of being interned in every concentration death camp that Hitler had ever built. After D-Day in 1944, the Allied forces slowly but surely liberated Europe. However, every time the Allies got close to liberating a concentration camp, the Nazi commanders would transfer Sam and other prisoners to another camp much deeper inside the Nazi-occupied territory. This enabled the Nazis to continue using them as slave labour which would keep the Nazi war machine alive as long as possible.

The last camp Sam was interned in was Bergen-Belsen, along with the incredible Anne Frank, who wrote her World-Famous diary, which became one of the most famous books of the 20th century.

Bergen-Belsen did not have gas chambers; however, the Nazis still managed to murder over 70,000 innocent people there between 1941 and 1945. During his time in the death camps, Sam and the other prisoners were abused all day and every day for years. With some being tortured to death in unimaginably perverse ways simply to amuse the vile Nazi commanders. They were also starved mercilessly, and when the camp was eventually liberated, over 13,000 bodies were found of people who had died from starvation alone.

During my interview with Sam, he said that he had eaten nothing except grass for over two weeks before the camp was finally liberated. How could anyone possibly maintain a positive mental attitude while enduring unimaginable horrors for years on end? Especially when there is no apparent hope in sight. The amazing Sam Rafowitz was one of the rare few who maintained his PMA.

When I asked him about this, he told me that targets were critical in remaining positive. He had set himself the target of staying alive for minutes, which eventually became an hour. He had set the same target to survive for another hour and eventually to survive to the end of the day. He would repeat the same process the following day and every day for five unimaginable years. He told me that each target he achieved always served to provide some positive feedback, even on his darkest days. He also focused on helping others, and in doing so, he learned how to make hats and gloves from the clothes of other prisoners who had died. These were essential items because the winters were brutally cold in central Europe, and the only clothes prisoners were given was a thin paper suit.

The 15th of April 1945 was the final day for Sam, and he was now so weak from lack of food that he could not even stand upright. He was lying in his prison hut on the bare wooden planks he used as a bed when he saw the Nazi guards assembling on the parade ground outside the window. Many hostages then thought that the Nazis were going to kill them before fleeing, but even at that unimaginably low point, Sam never lost hope. He always remained positive and focused entirely on survival and the hope of eventual liberation.

As Sam looked out of the prison hut window at the Nazi guards, he wondered what would happen next, and even if the guards would set the huts alight to burn them to death where they lay. Then, in the corner of his eye, he noticed something he had never seen before. It was a glimpse of something he had only dreamed about for the past five years. It was liberation.

He saw a British flag on a Jeep carrying a British Special Air Service (SAS) Officer, Lieutenant John Randall, and his driver. They were soon followed by tanks crashing through the gates of the prison camp, which were part of the British 11th Armoured Brigade. Very soon, British and Canadian troops were rounding up the Nazis, and medical teams were rushing to the aid of the prisoners.

Sam spent over six weeks in an army hospital with Nuns feeding him only sips of soup at a time until his body could digest regular food again. For the first few weeks, even though the much-dreamed-about liberation had finally come, it was still unclear if Sam would live or die. Even in this unimaginably weak condition, Sam remained positive and focused on living so that he might eventually find his sister. Sam and his sister had been separated at the time they were first interned in the concentration camps, and he was not even sure if she had lived through the hell of Nazi occupation. As always, Sam remained positive until it was proven otherwise.

Sam eventually recovered his health, and the Allied command gave him what they could spare in the way of clothing and money before he left as a free man once again. By chance, Sam found out that his sister had survived the war and was in Italy. This meant that for them to be reunited, he would have to cross the Alps, which is no easy thing to do, even with modern equipment.

Undeterred by 15,000-foot mountains stretching for over 750 miles across eight Alpine countries, Sam was as positively motivated as ever, so he set out to find his sister. It was a miracle how he did it because he had no Alpine clothing or equipment of any kind; he only had an old leather bag that he used to slide down the mountains on the snow. Through sheer determination, Sam made the crossing and eventually found his sister. Then, even more incredibly, they both crossed the Alps back to where Sam had started so he could bring her home. The first person they met after the second crossing was an American soldier of

Polish ethnicity who kindly helped them on their way. For the first time in years, they had hope in their hearts for a better future, and they literally tossed a coin to decide which country they would settle in.

Sam moved to the United States after the war ended, and as an immigrant, he used his hat and glove-making skills to help his family survive. With hard work and his amazing PMA, Sam used the skills he first learned when he was a prisoner in the concentration camps and turned them into a business. Fast-forward some 55 years, and to my first meeting with Sam. By this time, he had turned that small business into something big. He had grown a highly successful national company, which had helped many people in the process.

Sam Rafowitz is one of the most positively focused individuals I have ever met. He is also one of the most charming and delightful. Furthermore, he is a living testament to the power of having PMA as a guiding force that can bring you through the darkest times imaginable. The World is a much better place because of Sam Rafowitz's life, and I am truly honoured to know him.

After reading the true story of the amazing Sam Rafowitz and his incredible PMA, I can say that there is not much left that anyone can tell. How could anyone possibly doubt the power of having a positive mental attitude? More importantly, how can you ever complain about anything in your life ever again? How could you ever complain that you have had a tough week at work, have a long commute to work, or even complain pathetically that someone on Facebook was 'mean' to you? How can you ever say that you are feeling depressed and life is not great?

It is all about maintaining a realistic perspective. This is easy to say; however, it is not always easy to maintain in practice. This is because perspective is one of the most flexible things in the universe. It changes rapidly and without notice to fit neatly into different times in your life, like water changes shape to fit any size and shape of the container it is poured into. Therefore, maintaining a realistic perspective and maintaining a positive PMA are linked.

Self-Esteem

What is self-esteem? Good self-esteem generally means that you appreciate yourself and your worth. It means that you have a positive attitude, are certain of your abilities, and see yourself as being in control of all aspects of your life. Conversely, having poor self-esteem means being in the opposite state. In this state, you feel powerless to stand against life and all that it brings; perhaps you might even feel depressed because you have lost perspective. People with good self-esteem are more likely to succeed in social, business, and sporting activities. They are also less likely to engage in negative and self-destructive activities such as crime, drug abuse, and anti-social behaviour. Similar to respect, self-esteem must always be earned; it can never be given. Perhaps it could even be argued that self-esteem is a gift to yourself as a reward for hard and successful work.

Arrogance

There is a huge difference between arrogance and confidence. Genuine confidence is derived from quiet self-assuredness and courage, while arrogance arises from displaying and possessing an unwarranted and overbearing sense of self-importance. Those with arrogance also have an assumed feeling of superiority over others. The typical qualities associated with arrogance are:

- Arrogant people have a condescending attitude.
- Arrogant people are usually vain.
- Arrogant people have excessive, unhealthy pride.
- Arrogant people are often also narcissistic.
- Arrogant people are usually conceited.
- Arrogant people are usually expectant.
- Arrogant people have an over-inflated sense of entitlement.
- Arrogant people are often presumptuous.

In my opinion, arrogance combined with expectant entitlement are some of the most unappealing qualities a person could possess. These people never truly inspire others, nor do they make good leaders, because those they lead usually follow only because they must. Most importantly, arrogance usually completely blinds those people who possess this quality. They have no balanced sell-perspective whatsoever. It is almost laughable how these people can be so completely off-target in terms of their being able to accurately assess their ability to succeed or be genuinely good at something.

Unrealistic Expectation

Unrealistic expectations are becoming alarmingly common in the modern Western world. I believe that this is largely fueled by the misguided people who often control the media. The media often fosters unrealistic expectations, especially in the youth of the day, by suggesting that almost everyone can become a music star, a media star, or a sports star. It also suggests they can make fortunes in the process. Therefore, it should come as no surprise to anyone when young people drop out of school or choose to boycott higher education because of this misguided and dangerous propaganda.

As the great William Shakespeare once wrote:
"Expectation is the root of all heartache."

A surprisingly high proportion of people in the corporate world develop hugely unrealistic expectations as they rise through the ranks. They also often mistakenly begin to believe that working for a large company somehow qualifies them to run their own business. This is not necessarily true for all people. Working for a large company, even at a senior level, does not really prepare someone to set up a business and lead it effectively. There are always exceptions; however, they are extremely rare.

At times, you may engage opponents with unrealistic expectations, and in extreme cases, you may engage opponents who possess both narcissism and arrogance. I once gave intensive coaching to one of my closest friends when he faced an extreme example of the worst of 'all of the above.' Unfortunately, he had become romantically entangled with and then married to an extremely arrogant narcissist who also suffered from the most ridiculously unrealistic expectations. It was almost a textbook scenario of how to deal with such extreme opponents. Thankfully, we defeated his opponent, but not without him suffering some extreme emotional pain in the process.

Projectionist Syndrome

What I call Projectionist Syndrome can be surprisingly common. It can either be a mild annoyance or highly destructive; it depends on the severity of the syndrome and the overall psychosis of the person projecting. I believe the term Projectionist Syndrome could be paraphrased as 'projecting me, in you.' Furthermore, this is common when two people are in a long-term personal relationship. Perhaps the more common manifestations are found in small expressions of jealousy or in being particularly critical of another, usually about things that have no fundamental importance.

In most cases, that is as far as it goes. Even though it can annoy and perhaps even an occasional argument, it never usually goes any further. This is because it is tolerable and within certain boundaries of acceptability. However, this begs the question: Why do people project their negativity about themselves onto others?

According to Sigmund Freud, when a person projects their undesirable feelings, desires, thoughts, and even former actions onto another, it is all part of their defence mechanism. People project because there is something about themselves that they find deeply abhorrent, usually at a subconscious level. The deeper the abhorrence, the greater and more reinforced the projection becomes. The abhorrent things might be character flaws or wrongdoings from their present or past. The projection is usually subconscious, so the person projecting has no idea they are doing it.

Projectionist Syndrome is quite common in people who harbour deep-rooted guilt and negativity about themselves. Projecting onto another reduces their stress and guilt and makes them feel better without letting their conscious mind realise what is happening. I had never directly observed an extreme case of Projectionist Syndrome until I helped a close friend in his divorce battle with a partner who was also extremely arrogant and narcissistic. I was then able to observe an extreme case of the following abhorrent combination objectively:

- Extreme Narcissism.
- Extreme Arrogance.
- Extreme Unrealistic Expectations.
- Extreme Projectionist Syndrome.
- Extreme Linear Thinking.
- Extreme Lack of Common Business Sense.
- Extreme and Ridiculous Lies.

Narcissism

The narcissist can be one of the most frustrating and dangerous opponents to deal with. However, rest assured, they can be engaged and defeated using Mental Martial Arts.

The word narcissism comes from ancient Greek mythology. Narcissus was a handsome youth who rejected the advances of the nymph, Echo. As punishment by the Gods, he was doomed to fall in love with his reflection in a pool of water. Naturally, unable to consummate his love, Narcissus would do nothing except lie, gazing into the pool of water for hours on end. The legend tells that he eventually changed himself into a flower that still bears his name, the narcissus.

Narcissism is an unhealthy focus on one's 'self' that harms others. To a limited extent, we are all somewhat narcissistic, and this is perfectly normal when it is in proportion. After all, who does not want the good things in life? Psychologists tell us that everything we do is part of an emotional trade-off that enables us to feel better about ourselves and our lives. However, there is a huge difference between normal, healthy narcissism and destructive, self-consuming narcissism. Healthy narcissism is obtaining self-gratifying results in ways that do not damage other people. Conversely, unhealthy narcissism is the egotistical, complete preoccupation with oneself at the expense of all others. How others perceive them becomes the entire focus of their life.

Unhealthy narcissists lose their emotional contact and feelings with others until they reach a point where all they have left is a thin, ephemeral external veneer. These people are completely absorbed in themselves and are the centre of their universe. No matter how socially adept these people may appear to be on the surface, they have a significant attachment dysfunction.

I have encountered and engaged opponents with an unhealthy narcissistic disorder, and I have also coached others to deal with people like this. In doing so, I have seen how these people can change into various identities according to any given situation, which can make them almost like chameleons. This makes them particularly dangerous and not easy to identify initially. Often, on the surface, they can appear to be genuine, proper, courteous, and giving people. However, at their core, they are the antithesis of all these qualities.

I have also seen how, for my friend, a narcissist can be extremely destructive. Narcissistic people will remain close to their partners only as long as they are useful. Then, like a swarm of locusts, their partner will usually be discarded like a piece of old junk once they have taken all they wanted. At the same time, they might even attempt to bring more focus upon themselves as somehow being wronged. Make no mistake, these people are extremely dangerous, so here are some indicators to help you spot a narcissist:

- Narcissists react strongly to criticism with anger or with other outward emotional expressions.
- Narcissists take advantage of people, and they coldly use others to help them reach their targets.
- Narcissists usually brag about themselves, sometimes in ways that are cleverly concealed. They usually grossly exaggerate their importance, achievements, and talents.
- Narcissists require almost constant attention, feeding off the positive reinforcement of those around them.
- Narcissists can be very jealous, sometimes in very subtle ways.
- Narcissists are completely emotionally detached from the feelings of others, often disregarding them completely.
- Narcissists are often incapable of empathy and usually display subtle tell-tale signs of being unemotional.
- Narcissists are obsessed with themselves.
- Narcissists have problems gaining and then maintaining healthy relationships.
- Narcissists often set unrealistic goals based entirely upon their imagined persona's ability.
- Narcissists usually want to be seen to have the best of everything.
- Narcissists are usually bullies, yet they are always the first to complain if anyone even comes close to bullying them.

The important points to remember when engaging a narcissistic opponent are:

- Lead them to believe they are at the centre of your thoughts, decisions, and everything. Offer them as much praise as you can.
- Provide constant positive feedback to distract them as you engage, and then lead them in a direction of your choice.
- Outright refusal of anything they want or suggest typically completely deflates them. This will then lead them to be more controlled by you without them realising it.
- As soon as your Chi Sau senses that your narcissist opponent is asserting themselves and is developing rage, then simply walk away. Ignore them and behave with complete disregard for them

as if they did not exist. Remember that a narcissist cannot fight an opponent they do not have.

Building Self-Confidence and Healthy Self-Esteem

Having total belief in yourself will have an enormous impact on how others will perceive you, especially since you only have about 90 seconds to make an excellent first impression when you meet someone new. Furthermore, since a person's perception is always their reality, the more you believe in the real you, the more others will believe in you, too. It becomes a sort of self-fulfilling process. You can do several things to help speed up both building and maintaining a solid base of self-confidence. Here are some essential confidence-building tips.

Exercise

Anthropologically, humans are designed to be physically active. However, thanks to our modern and increasingly sedentary lifestyle, we should be more conscious than ever before of our level of physical fitness and diet. Physical fitness has a positive effect on self-confidence because if you are fit and in good shape, you will naturally exude greater confidence than if you were out of shape and overweight. If you have the budget, then join a gym or take workout classes. However, if your budget is tight, buy a new or used Bullworker total-body personal multi-gym home exerciser. A new one is in the region of £/$ 250, and second-hand, circa £/$ 50-150, with a good selection of instruction manuals available online or through Amazon. Furthermore, the Bullworker unisex personal multi-gym is an incredibly versatile and effective device that some of the finest professional athletes in the world swear by.

Take Good Posture

Your posture will express to others how you feel about yourself. Therefore, if you take and maintain a consistently good posture, you will not only feel better by doing so but also look better and feel more confident. Think about a movie where the actor portrays a person with low self-confidence and low self-esteem. How do they physically look? How do they stand and express themselves? You will see the actor with slumped shoulders and using slow, lethargic movements. Therefore, you should stand up straight, keep your head up and make direct eye contact with others.

Walk Well

Using the movies as a medium of objective observation, think about an actor portraying someone with little or no self-confidence. Think about how that actor might walk. In such a role, they would naturally walk slowly and lethargically, almost dragging their feet as they do so. They would never portray such a character by walking upright, briskly, with direction, energy, and zest. Confident people usually walk slightly more quickly than those who are less confident. Therefore, even if you are not necessarily in a hurry, simply walking a little faster will naturally make you feel better and, in turn, slightly more confident.

Dress Well

The old saying that clothes maketh the man is not entirely true because they also maketh the woman. Dressing well will undoubtedly make you feel better about yourself under any circumstances. This is a personal statement, your expression to the world about what comprises the inner you. Simply put, if you do not look good, you will not feel good. What you wear and how you wear it will speak volumes about you and tell the world how you feel about yourself.

It is important to remember that you should always wear high-quality clothes which fit well. Quality clothes usually have the added advantage of lasting longer, too. If you wear high-quality garments, it naturally follows that you should also wear high-quality shoes. Shoes are one of the best indicators of the overall quality of your appearance. To wear high-quality clothes combined with shoddy, low-quality shoes only makes the observer doubt your overall success. Simply wearing great shoes is an incredible confidence booster. Senior politicians and executives all dress well. They dress powerfully, and their clothes exude quality, which, in turn, helps to create their confident image and powerful charisma.

It is a better strategy to buy fewer clothes and shoes, but of better quality. Quality items usually remain in style for years, and you will end up with a lot less jumble in your life and wardrobe. It is also a good idea to ensure that your clothes and shoes are always neat, clean, fresh, well-pressed, and ironed. If your budget is tight and goodwill/charity stores are your primary source of clothes and shoes, use public transport to visit more affluent areas. There, the goodwill/charity stores will have donated some of the highest quality brand names, often unworn and sold for a bargain price.

Straight Down the Middle

This might sound just like a line from a song, and indeed it is. However, in this instance, I am not referring to golf as the great Bing Crosby did in his classic song of the same name. I am referring to how you physically move in life. For example, those who lack self-confidence will often enter a conference room using a side door or while screened slightly behind others as they attempt to enter the room unnoticed.

Once inside the auditorium, they usually find a seat located at or near the rear, where, once again, they believe they will remain relatively unnoticed. Conversely, those who are confident will do the exact opposite. They will often enter the auditorium by simultaneously opening both double doors. They will usually walk straight down the middle of the room and sit at the front or as close to the front as possible. By their actions alone, they are making a clear statement to others in the room that they are confident and assertive. The question is, what kind of a statement do you want to make about yourself?

Your Elevator Speech

An excellent way to build confidence is to practice your Elevator Speech. The Elevator Speech refers to the possibility of delivering a presentation or an idea in the time it takes for an average elevator ride. This would usually be a maximum of 30 seconds, consisting of around 130 words or less. This is the typical time you have when presenting an idea to a board of directors at a meeting. You have just 30 seconds to present yourself in a concise, coherent, and complete presentation to persuade others about yourself and your idea. An effective Elevator Speech to summarise what you offer will not only teach you how to present yourself well to others when required, but it will also reinforce your strengths and qualities. In turn, this will increase your self-confidence in the process.

Chapter 9 Summary – Power Moves:

- 武 *Total belief and self-confidence become your perception and reality.*
- 武 *Recognise and remember the differences between confidence and arrogance.*

Chapter 9 Summary – Pressure Points:

- 武 *Exercise, good posture, and walking well will help to create a more confident 'you'.*
- 武 *Buy fewer, but better, clothes and shoes to ensure that you always dress powerfully.*
- 武 *Some people project their flaws, feelings, and reality of 'self' onto others.*
- 武 *Devise your Elevator Speech. This will help maintain a positive self-image and enhance the perception of yourself to others.*

Chapter 10: Leadership

The great Shaolin Masters teach:
"From humility comes forth good Leadership."

Therefore, this begs the question: What exactly is good leadership? The concept of leadership has been studied for centuries, and many schools of thought have existed about it. Therefore, I will examine some concepts and qualities related to leaders and leadership. A good leader is usually easily recognised. However, it is much harder to understand exactly what it takes to become a good leader. I believe that all people are born with certain leadership qualities, but not everyone chooses to develop or exercise them. Leadership seems to be a quality you know instantly when you see it, despite often being difficult to define and describe.

Sun Tzu, one of the greatest leaders of all time, shared his thoughts in his famous book 'The Art of War.' This is also one of the oldest known military texts, dated circa 400 BC, and its essence is basically about how to fight wars without having to fight a battle. He recommended that leaders outwit opponents so that physical conflict was unnecessary. This is the same underpinning philosophy my Shaolin Masters taught me, and is the underpinning philosophy of Mental Martial Arts. The Art of War and Sun Tzu's philosophy have become revered in the West by military leaders, political leaders, corporate leaders, world-class sports team managers, and the legal profession. The teachings of Sun Tzu and The Art of War have even become required reading in many of the world's leading business schools. Therefore, it seems that those in positions of power in the West are finally realising the value of ancient Eastern philosophies in benefiting good leadership.

Quote:
"Glory is for the historians to decide and ponder upon because there is no glory in being a leader."

When thinking about a leader, most people think first about the status and elevated position that comes with leadership. They rarely give a second thought to the enormous amount of hard work, dedication, loneliness, agony, study, and determination that went into creating that person as a leader. The much-admired leadership position came at the expense of all the above and more.

As with all positions of great power, leadership and responsibility go hand in hand. The leadership factor often attracts criticism, mockery, and even attacks about a leader's character and private life. In fact, such things should be expected by those in any leadership role.

Since leadership is often highly challenging, why do people agree to undertake such a role? Obviously, there are as many reasons as there are individuals. However, the main reasons are usually integrity, courage, passion, and a sense of duty. Those who are natural leaders do not usually seek to become leaders; they simply are leaders. It is also possible for others who seek to become leaders to learn leadership qualities and the factors that foster good leadership.

In certain situations, some people will naturally become the leader, usually because of a problem or crisis. It is either the natural choice at the time or the way it happens for whoever becomes the leader. These people rapidly shift almost instantly from relative invisibility into the highly visible realm of being under the leadership spotlight.

This is usually the result of unfolding events, and because of those people's responses to those events. Furthermore, the unwitting person who has undertaken the role of leader is suddenly responsible for many new things. Perhaps it is the success of an event that is at stake or even the entire livelihood of those they lead. Either way, it is still an enormous responsibility.

Most people want someone else to make the first move and take the lead in almost all aspects of life. Most people are much happier as followers than as leaders. To see this phenomenon in action, observe any group during a team-building session. You will immediately see that most people will automatically assume the follower role. There is absolutely nothing wrong with this because not everyone can be a leader, and if they were, then there would be no one to lead. Therefore, the most apparent factor in leadership is that any leader must have followers; otherwise, they will only lead themselves.

To be an effective leader, you need more than followers; you also need the complete support of those who follow you. Without this crucial factor, your leadership will be, at worst, completely useless and, at best, ineffectual. This then begs the question: Why are leaders followed? The main reason is that those who follow trust and respect the leader as an individual, not just for the skills they possess. In short, the leader must have influenced the followers in one or more ways.

Leaders are usually highly driven, passionate, and target-oriented, and they usually possess great clarity of vision. The best leaders are also usually excellent strategic planners and can envision things in a multidimensional and tactical way. This is hugely different from the more usual linear thinking methods employed by those following the leader.

Good leaders are adaptive and exceptionally creative. They must be able to produce innovative solutions to seemingly impossible problems. They always take ownership of whatever they are doing and drive it to success. Moreover, good leaders never lose focus on their target while guiding, supporting, and nurturing their followers. Therefore, effective leadership is more focused on behaviour, trust, and a charismatic personality rather than on the more traditionally valued qualities of being able to manage tasks. Therefore, there is often a huge difference between management and leadership roles.

Managers and Leaders

A manager organises a series of tasks and processes, which is quite different from what a leader does. Just because someone has proven they can manage things well does not automatically make them a good leader. However, the roles of manager and leader often go hand in hand as part of the job.

To some degree, all those selected to manage must have at least some degree of leadership ability, and some managers excel more at leading than managing. The reality is that good leaders are not necessarily good managers, and good managers are not necessarily natural strategists or good leaders. Managers are often promoted into the role because they are exceptionally process-focused individuals. Since managers almost always display at least the basic characteristics of good leadership, with proper coaching, they may also become exceptional leaders. Alternatively, some achieve management status and are also naturally gifted and exceptional leaders. These people just need the right opportunity to prove their leadership abilities to the world.

I believe that organisations should invest much more in the professional development training of their managers because they are essential to the success of any organisation. Furthermore, enhancing their already proven management abilities with advanced leadership training makes good business sense.

Styles, Characters, and Flaws

Leadership, style, and personal character are very much horns on the same beast. This is because the leadership style is usually an extension of the individual's personal character. A person's character is generally derived from a combination of past experiences, skills, personality, values, and principles. Character is formed over a long period, starting in early childhood, with a person's words and deeds determining their ultimate morality. Therefore, a person's character will influence and ultimately determine a person's actions. If a person's character is known or if it can become known, then the motivation and the targets of that person will also become known. Knowing your opponent and yourself is an instrumental factor contributing to your overall success.

Many managers and leaders are fortunate to display a well-balanced character. However, many do not, and often have the people they lead wondering how on earth they ever got the job. Some people can shape and morph their character to fit the needs required in certain situations. These people are character chameleons, and in the right circumstances, they can make exceptional leaders.

Character flaws usually restrict a person's long-term success, and such people are usually easily dealt with as opponents. You should always seek to use their chief character flaw against them. This is always their Achilles heel because whatever a person believes to be their greatest strength will also be their greatest weakness. Your great advantage in all this is that such people usually do not see any weakness in themselves. Even the best leaders have character flaws, which are powerful weapons if you ever engage and need to defeat an opponent who is in a leadership position. You can use these brief character vignettes to help you plan your strategy.

武 Arrogance

You combat arrogance by using a person's arrogance against them. Such people are usually predictable, and their arrogance typically overrides their good sense.

武 Narcissism

Narcissism and arrogance often go hand in hand. These people can be powerful opponents because they are often completely ruthless. Remember, these people are even more predictable than those who are merely arrogant. Lead them into believing they are in complete control, and then feed their thirst for praise as well as their need to be revered. Use patience, remove your ego from the equation, and you can engineer their downfall.

武 Status Driven

A status-driven individual will usually hesitate when making difficult decisions. They are always driven by the status of what they do and by what they are seen to be doing. This is a serious weakness, and it can be effectively used against them, especially since they are usually completely unaware of it.

武 Aggression

You combat aggression by causing an aggressive or ill-tempered person to be impulsive and rash. You want them to lose their temper and become angry. In this condition, such people almost always instinctively react rather than respond. Since their reactions are usually predictable, you can use this knowledge against them.

武 Cavalier Attitude

You can effectively engage a person with a cavalier attitude by causing such a person to uselessly waste their resources. Given time, they will usually do this of their own volition, so just help them with the process. These people usually display certain characteristics of arrogance, which helps to make them highly predictable.

武 Nervous

If a person is nervous, then they should take the moral high ground and play it safe. Ask as many relevant questions as you wish, and as you do so, work to increase their fears. Make them fear everything in every decision they must make by creating metaphoric ghosts, shadows, and demons at every turn.

Strong Leaders Build Strong Teams

As a rule, if the person leading a team is weak, then the team will usually be weak, insubordinate, and ineffective. They will waste time and energy debating issues that should not even need to be debated. Eventually, committee mentality will develop, which makes them extremely slow to respond to change and opportunity, no matter how urgently it might be needed.

If a team leader is incompetent, then the team will be generally mismanaged. Their strategies will be poor, and their losses in terms of finance and opportunity will usually be significant. Their relationships with sub-team leaders under their command will eventually become strained, and the leader will become increasingly disorganised.

I have also witnessed how some of the best leaders are also regularly passed over for promotion. In some cases, they cannot even get basic employment. This usually happens because the chain of management within an organisation has become weak and possibly inert. They will be either consciously or subconsciously frightened about employing anyone who they consider might become a threat to their position.

Fear can be a huge problem in leadership, especially for those who lack confidence in themselves. Their fears will be further increased and driven by their hidden shortcomings and inadequacies. They will fear any newcomer, especially someone who is more talented than they are. They will become increasingly concerned that they will be exposed as being nothing more than 'paper tigers' and people who do not really deserve the job.

Weak recruiters such as these are killing their organisation from within. If they genuinely wanted to make their organisation stronger and more profitable, they would always seek to employ only the best people possible, even if the newcomers are better than they are. Furthermore, this would be the absolute best way to safeguard their jobs.

The Shaolin Masters teach:

"One must first understand and embrace humility, with all its facets, to become a truly great leader."

Leadership styles

There are many different styles of leadership that have been well documented. There are as many different styles of leadership as there are leaders. Since every person is unique, they will naturally develop their signature leadership style. However, no matter what their leadership style might be, they will still always fall into one or more of the documented categories.

All the leadership styles I have listed below have self-explanatory names, making it easy to identify the characteristic style of leadership they represent. I have started my list with two very well-known yet opposite styles of leadership from the hit TV series Star Trek and Star Trek: The Next Generation. The latter is a TV show that I once worked on in the late 1980s.

- The Captain Kirk Style of Leader.
- The Captain Picard Style of Leader.
- The Leader by Example.
- The Bureaucratic Leader.
- The Easy-Going Leader.
- The Charismatic Leader.
- The Performance-Oriented Leader.
- The Autocratic Leader.
- The Encouraging Leader.
- The True-Grit Style of Leader.
- The People-Oriented Leader.
- The Happy Leader.
- The Task-Oriented Leader.
- The Servant to Others Style of Leader.
- The Transformational Leader.
- The Environmental Leader.
- The Dictatorial Leader.
- The Democratic Leader.

A good exercise would be to take each of the classifications of leadership styles I have listed above and then make notes about the thoughts and feelings you have towards each of them. Make specific notes about the various strengths and weaknesses you associate with each. Once you have completed your notes, list those people in leadership roles whom you know personally, and then determine what category each would fit into according to your list. Finally, the most challenging task of all will be to objectively evaluate your leadership style in the same way to see where you believe you would fit in.

In the words of my great friend and IT guru, Lynn Carnes, the former Senior Vice President of Wells Fargo Bank:

"Organisations take on the characteristics of their leaders. So, if you encounter organisations that are difficult to deal with, which are weak, ineffectual, or aggressive, then you have the true measure of the leadership."

Elements of Leadership

If good leadership is about attributes of behaviour such as trust and charisma, then if you intend to develop leadership qualities, you should aim to develop similar behaviours and characteristics. Psychologists tell us that leaders oriented toward short-term targets differ in style and character from leaders focused on the longer term. To recap, short-term thinkers are usually left-brain dominant, as opposed to long-term thinkers who are typically right-brain dominant. Those who can switch between the two or sit squarely in the middle almost always make the greatest leaders. Great leaders are not always the ones with the best academic qualifications. Gaining a degree or a similar higher-level qualification merely demonstrates the ability to read, rationalise, and linearly remember facts. Exceptional leaders are often non-linear, sometimes even elliptical in their thoughts. The list below contains some of the qualities and elements of character possessed by and associated with good leaders.

- 武 A good leader can motivate people.
- 武 A good leader has great courage and resolve.
- 武 A good leader will begin planning to find their successor as soon as they take the leadership role.
- 武 A good leader will usually under-promise and over-deliver.

- A good leader will only promise what they can guarantee to deliver.
- A good leader is adaptive and flexible, able to improvise with ease whenever needed.
- A good leader completely supports those who follow them.
- A good leader usually possesses great physical energy, stamina, and endurance.
- A good leader is Intelligent, usually displaying a mix of left and right-brain thinking.
- A good leader is oriented towards action while being tempered by good judgment.
- A good leader has a clear understanding of those who follow them.
- A good leader has great skills in dealing with people.
- A good leader always gives those they lead the credit for success; they never take the credit themselves.
- A good leader will constantly seek to learn from the people around them.
- A good leader has an inbuilt desire to achieve.
- A good leader is trustworthy.
- A good leader is always decisive.
- A good leader always maintains the highest integrity.
- A good leader is completely competent at the job.
- A good leader is self-confident and never arrogant.
- A good leader is assertive but never aggressive.
- A good leader is never self-promoting.
- A good leader is firm and clear when dealing with bad or unethical behaviour.

A good leader will never publicly blame another person for failing. If someone they led has failed, they will take the blame themselves. They will then diligently coach the person who has failed so that person will eventually succeed. The qualities which make a great leader are within most people, and they simply need to search deep enough within themselves to find them.

Leadership and Team Building

Good leaders understand that the success of their team always depends on the individuals who comprise the team. Even the best team must be coached, mentored, and steered in the same direction. It must be focused on a common target while working in a coordinated, cooperative, and efficient way.

During the 1980s and 1990s, companies recognised team building as a major factor in producing good employee cooperation within their organisation. It was also proven to help companies remain commercially competitive even in tough economic markets. Today, we live in a commercial world that is evolving and changing faster than ever before. Therefore, I believe that team building is more important to an organisation than ever. Unfortunately, short-sighted organisations often mistakenly believe that team building is a luxury, something better suited to more stable economic times. Nothing could be further from the truth. When times are tough, organisations need to rely on the quality and motivation of their teams more than ever. Therefore, to cut back on the thing they need the most is corporate insanity. The enormous benefits of effective team building include:

- Increased communication skills.
- Establishing common targets, defining roles and responsibilities, and learning cross-tasking.
- Building greater mutual trust.
- Group and interpersonal bonding are greatly improved.
- Learning new skills and techniques.
- Learning to improvise, adapt, and overcome obstacles by employing lateral thinking methods.
- Helping to overcome the fears and phobias of certain team members.
- The increased feeling of value and self-worth.
- FUN!

If you are ever required to build a team, then personal coaching and mentoring will be essential. You do not need a title or position to give your leadership justification or worth. Good leadership comes from your deeds, never from simply words alone. It also has great clarity of vision and little regard for fear. Great leaders do not need to beat people to lead them; instead, they will naturally inspire and encourage others.

Catherine the Great of Russia once said, *"I praise loudly, I blame softly."*

These are wise words. However, in my opinion, the Shaolin Master's words are the wisest of all as they teach us to:

"Be more afraid of an army of doves led by a tiger than an army of tigers led by a dove."

Chapter 10 Summary – Power Moves:

- 武 One must first understand and embrace humility, with all its facets, to become a truly great leader.
- 武 The public face of any company or organisation is always a direct reflection of the leadership.
- 武 Teamwork is essential in life, love, and business.

Chapter 10 Summary – Pressure Points:

- 武 Managers are an asset to any organisation, and they deserve a greater investment in their training.
- 武 The right selection process for any leader is critical.
- 武 There are many leadership styles; however, every leader is still unique.
- 武 Just because someone is loud or bullying, it does not make them a good leader.
- 武 Teamwork increases essential communication skills.
- 武 Good teamwork is essential to all organisations, no matter how large or small. It creates and helps to maintain a highly motivated workforce.

Chapter 11: Toolboxes and Tactics

Let's explore the 'Toolbox Tactics' concept, a phrase I coined that resonates well with the people I've coached. This principle, rooted in basic common sense, forms the bedrock of effective business practices.

Imagine for a moment that you are a student of kung fu in ancient China, leading a team of newly trained Shaolin warriors into battle. The toolbox you have at your disposal to fight this battle comprises the skills of the trained warriors, weapons, ammunition, terrain, and the element of surprise, etc. You would have a great many tools at your disposal, all of which can be used in a multitude of different ways.

As the leader, the choice of exactly how they are used is entirely up to you. If you make serious errors in using any one of the elements, then you may be defeated. Conversely, if you use the elements wisely and strategically as a good leader, then you may even win the battle without having to fight.

The difference between victory and defeat is not what tools you have at your disposal; it is always how you choose to use them. During the 40+ years I have spent studying physical martial arts, I have experienced countless combat sessions. Some were in training, some in competition, and some were in real self-defence situations. Every time I was about to engage in combat, I would always evaluate my opponent's strengths and weaknesses.

At the same time, I always tried to maximise the use of every available weapon I had at my disposal. More importantly, I always knew that there was always a multitude of different combinations in how each weapon could be used. This was my toolbox, and what I did with the tools in it and the combinations I used were always going to be my choice.

In life, love, and business, we all have a multitude of tools at our disposal. If we choose to use these tools in a specific combination and with a certain strategy, then a particular outcome will be the result. If one or more of the tools are changed, if you change the way the tools are used, or if your strategy and tactics change, then a different outcome will be the result. It is just like using a recipe when cooking food. Change any one of the ingredients, change how each ingredient is used, and a different result will be produced every time.

Ultimately, the power lies with you. You are the one who determines how each tool in your life, love, and business is used. You are the captain of your life's ship, the ultimate decision-maker. Hence, you hold the reins of your fate.

- The career path you follow.
- What income will you earn?
- What kind of love life will you enjoy?

Another excellent example of how the same toolbox might be used differently would be to take three identical sets of paint and brushes. Then, give each set to three different people. One person may take those materials and paint their house, producing a pleasant but straightforward result. Another person may take an identical set of paint and brushes and do nothing more than paint graffiti in public places. A person like Michelangelo would have an identical set of paint and brushes to create the incredible paintings of the Sistine Chapel. The toolbox might be the same, but the key difference is always the person using the tools.

Most people from similar walks of life have similar tools at their disposal in their toolbox of life. Some people may have slightly more of one element and less of another, but generally, there is always some comparative balance. The critical thing to remember is that you can take the elements in your toolbox, and when combined with a creative mind, you can achieve just about any realistic target you choose to set.

I am always disappointed when people complain, blaming others for their lack of success or opportunity. It is ridiculous to blame others for something which you are in complete control of. If you do not achieve the desired results in life, love, or business, then use the tools you have at your disposal differently. It is that simple. Start again, using a different combination of tools and with a different recipe. Just dare to believe that you can achieve whatever you truly desire.

My father once taught me:
"Remember, son, if one person can achieve something in life, then you can too."

Self-Sabotage

We all possess a range of simple tools which can help prevent self-sabotage. However, many people seem to be programmed for self-sabotage because they fear the success they are supposed to desire. I am going to briefly examine some of the reasons why certain people choose to self-sabotage and fail.

Since people choose to self-sabotage and fail mainly because of the fear of success, I have often wondered why they cannot be more easily identified in advance. This is probably because their fear does not typically manifest itself at a conscious level. However, it is real and almost always produces the failure they secretly desire. Since these people are hard to spot, they make it incredibly challenging to select the right business partners. No matter what tools these people have at their disposal, they will typically find a way to sabotage their success.

This character flaw primarily manifests itself in those who have confidence and control issues and those who have difficulty handling change. These people will always like the concept of whatever they attempt to achieve, but they would always prefer to preserve their current status quo. Some people may even enjoy the attention they receive from those expressing support after a well-attempted failure. Such people will always let it be widely known that the element which caused them to fail was entirely beyond their control, and they never take ownership of it themselves.

More importantly, look out for the signs of self-sabotage in your nature because we can all express elements of this flaw. Examine the times when you have not initially achieved the success you desired. Did any self-sabotage elements in your character enter the equation? If you detect any of these characteristics, work to eliminate them using the caveat technique and positive self-talk to help reprogram your mind.

Perfectionist Syndrome

Perfectionist syndrome is another common form of self-sabotage. Perfectionists create countless excuses for not being quite ready to start on whatever course of action they have set themselves. These people are initially seen as detail-oriented and are often commended for that. However, their attention to detail continually delays them from embarking on their journey. For these people, it is just never quite the right time for them to finally start.

They often choose to debate at length the fine details of colours, tones, shapes, designs, etc., all of which are subconscious ploys to help them delay starting something. When there are no more excuses to delay their start, they often find that the world has passed them by, and the window of opportunity has disappeared. If these people are in the start-up phase of a business, then it is not uncommon for them to run out of money long before they are finally willing to start trading.

I would never disagree with anyone about the importance of paying close attention to detail. However, there is a big difference between having proper attention to detail and getting lost somewhere in perfectionist syndrome.

The primary objective in business is to make money and generate cash flow. If you constantly procrastinate about starting trading, then this will never happen. Perfectionist syndrome is driven by fear. A common fear is that failure in business is always a possibility, and those with an inflated ego and narcissistic issues would have a real problem with this.

After all, narcissists always believe that they are already the best at everything. Therefore, if there is an element of doubt about their ability at a subconscious level, then this will cause conflict within them. Beware of any signs and symptoms of perfectionist syndrome in your character, especially in your business or potential business partners. After all, you are never really in business until you start trading with your customers.

An ancient Shaolin proverb teaches:

"Water takes the path of least resistance; it never seeks to flow uphill. Let your success strategies do the same, avoid what is difficult, and seek the easier path."

Anchors Are Tools

Anchor points are basically strong associations which vividly remind us of certain feelings and experiences. These can be handy tools because your association with a specific anchor can make all the difference between feeling happy and sad, positive or negative. More importantly, using anchors and their positive associations can make all the difference between success and failure. Anchors are especially valuable when you are under extreme stress and in crisis. They can also be helpful in daily life and business to maintain continuous subliminal positive assurances and reinforcement.

I have extensive experience using anchor points to help friends and clients in crises, so I understand how important they are. I also know, through experience, their value in sports and fields of human endeavour.

For example, two good friends and I share an appreciation of the bagpipes. The bagpipes have grown to represent much more than just a musical instrument for all three of us. They are a solid anchor point that, at times, has made the difference between happiness and sadness, courage and despair, and success and failure.

One of these people was the twice-world martial arts champion, the former King of Thailand's Thai Boxing champion, with 169 undefeated fights in Thailand and around the Far East. Stuart Hurst is from my hometown of Manchester, England. We have been as close as brothers for 45+ years and are training partners in the martial arts and for strength events.

Curiously, we both shared a love of the bagpipes and what they represent has been highly significant to our success in our chosen sport. Stuart and I have made some of our best lifts in powerlifting and achieved some of our greatest successes in martial arts, with the music of the bagpipes as a positive anchor point.

Another friend who shares this anchor association and love of the bagpipes is the amazing Bill Kazmaier, considered by many to be the strongest man who ever lived. Search on the internet for "Pure Strength '87", and you will see Bill at Huntley Castle in Scotland competing against my other friends, Jon Pall Sigmarsson and the legendary Geoff Capes. While we were at Huntley Castle, Bill and I learned that we had a shared love of the pipes. We both agreed that they were a key motivator for each of us, especially when we needed to summon up our reserves of strength.

Bill told me that he always feels stronger and more motivated when the pipers are playing, and his incredible feats of strength prove it.

I was never even close to being in the same league as Bill, Geoff, or Jon Pall, but this anchor association worked amazingly well for me on many occasions. When Bill was competing to win back his title of World's Strongest Man, in an interview, he even said that he can always lift more weight when the bagpipes are playing tunes such as 'The Black Bear,' 'Highland Laddie,' or 'Scotland the Brave.' This is a perfect example of how a simple anchor can help to motivate someone to become the World's Strongest Man. If they can work for him at that level, they can work for all of us in our chosen field of endeavour.

When thinking about anchor points, many people also think about Ivan Petrovich Pavlov, the famous Russian physiologist who won the Nobel Prize in 1904. Pavlov contributed mainly to the fields of physiology and neurological sciences and became most famous for his concept of 'conditioned reflex.'

Pavlov discovered something highly significant during his experiments with dogs and their responsive salivation. When a bell was rung, and a dog was given food within a certain time, the animal would salivate when it saw the food. The dog would eventually come to associate the ringing of the bell with being given food, and from that point forward, it would salivate simply upon hearing the bell.

This is a fundamental anchor point because it is a stimulus that calls forth a particular state of mind, specific emotions and thoughts, etc. This is also sometimes called 'event pairing', where a particular event triggers a response.

We all have anchor points that we rarely give a second thought to, and these anchor points always represent extremely specific things to each of us. They could be certain tunes you associate with a particularly happy time in your life or specific smells, such as fresh coffee, that take you back to the happy days of childhood. It does not matter what the anchor point is; the fact is that each anchor point always triggers a certain response.

Anchor points can trigger positive and negative responses, which is why someone might be perfectly happy one moment and then suddenly become sad for no reason. This is simply because they have unexpectedly encountered a particular anchor point that triggers a sad response.

Most of our anchor points have been created organically over the years as we grow as human beings through life experiences. However, there are other kinds of anchor points, which I call decided anchor points. By using decided anchor points as a tool, you can provide yourself with a self-generated support mechanism that can provide confidence, positive motivation, and an increased state of happiness whenever you need it.

How do you create fixed anchor points? The process is quite simple. Begin by determining precisely what state you wish to anchor; for this example, it can be the state of happiness. Then, choose the anchor or anchors you want to associate with that state. The anchors can be anything you wish; they can be an object, a simple touch of your hand, a tune, a smell, or the memory of a certain person.

It does not matter what it is, just so long as it is positive and important to you. It should also be easy to trigger when needed. Next, close your eyes and envision a specific time in your life when you were experiencing the state you wish to anchor. Think about a time when you were extremely happy and examine every element of your recollection of that time. Examine the sights, sounds, smells, tastes, and even what certain things feel like to the touch.

When you reach the peak of your desired state in envisioning something specific, think about the anchors you wish to associate with it. As always, the more detail you can include in your vision, the better and more effective the process will be. When the images fade as you eventually fall into a more relaxed post-envisionment state, keep applying the anchor to the detail for as long as possible.

Finally, take a deep breath and, with your eyes still closed, count down from 10 to zero. Take several deep and calming breaths as you do so. When you reach zero, open your eyes and deliberately distract yourself back into the now. This process should be repeated several times, and each time you do so, try to make the experience even more vivid and detailed. Once your anchor point is established, regular use will continue to reinforce it and firmly embed it into your mind.

Maximise Meetings

Meetings are extremely useful tools if you know how to maximise them. They are typically used to efficiently discuss issues, disseminate information, or gather collective thoughts.

However, there are other strategic uses for meetings when engaged in a conflict situation. Under such conditions, a series of meetings could be scheduled, yet each meeting would be cancelled at the very last moment using a plausible excuse. This tactic and good timing can help buy you time and significantly destabilise your opponent. It can even make them angry and frustrated. This can be a good thing because anger and frustration are the enemies of sound judgment. Anger is also an emotion that tends to invoke a reaction rather than a calculated response. This generally makes it good for you and bad for your opponent.

It is essential to first learn how to accurately judge whether a meeting is really needed. You may be confusing activity with accomplishment. Calling an unnecessary meeting will simply waste time and resources. When considering convening a meeting, first take a strategic overview of precisely why you wish to do so. Consider your overall objectives together with the best use of time for all those who would be involved. Then, if a meeting is needed, arrange one.

If you are not already well acquainted with the people you are meeting with, it is vital to gather as much information as possible before the meeting takes place. You should also gather as much information about their organisation as possible. It is always worth researching their finances, new products, permissions to build new property, etc. The more information you have, the better prepared you will be.

For example, you may want to buy a building from a small company, but your information about their finances suggests they need to free up cash quickly. In that case, the 'string-along-meeting' approach should be used to draw out the time spent in negotiation. With meeting after meeting taking place and with you continuing to ask relevant questions that might take time to answer in detail, this will draw out the time before a conclusion can be reached.

This will also significantly affect their original estimation of when the deal would be complete and give them the money from the sale. If they are out of their financial comfort zone, they will get nervous about a deal and how, if it fails, it will leave them in a time crunch while searching for another buyer. You might get what you want at a much better price than initially anticipated.

The cancellation technique is also a handy tactic. Convening a meeting and then cancelling at the last moment will always help to destabilise an opponent. This technique is even more effective if you have regularly exchanged a lot of information with your opponent before the proposed meeting. Detailed communication with an opponent before a meeting will build up their anticipation, while the sudden and unexpected cancellation will provide a colossal let-down.

With good strategic timing, this technique can work to your advantage, and it can help you gain the additional leverage you need to close a better deal in your favour. It can influence costs and the timing of your final commitment, and it can even provide you with an acceptable get-out option just in case it is needed. The technique can generate an abrupt cancellation of the whole deal by the other party. There are times when this might be the more desirable option, especially if you have already decided that you do not wish to complete the deal but would prefer your opponent to cancel instead of you.

You also need to learn what factors always override the meeting in terms of importance, so that if needed, you can cancel well in advance and prevent wasting people's time. Too many meetings are convened simply for the sake of convening a meeting. Perhaps some are more about boosting the team's confidence rather than sharing information and ideas. This is more prevalent when both the convenor and the team lack confidence and experience.

One of the biggest annoyances is calling a company to buy something and then being told that the salesperson you need to deal with is in a sales meeting and cannot come to the phone. There are occasions when the whole business world seems locked in a cycle of continuous meetings instead of working and doing business with clients. 'Meeting Mentality is an interesting phenomenon many organisations suffer from.

An excellent example occurred several years ago with a company that used to be my main broadcast TV video equipment supplier. Things were fine until a new sales manager took over. After that, even something as simple as trying to get hold of someone in the sales department became highly challenging.

My own company had just secured a contract to supply a department of the local government with a package of video equipment and professional development training. However, there was a deadline connected with the deal. I also knew that some of the lead times to source the video equipment from the manufacturers could be highly frustrating. I called my supply company as soon as the deal had been signed, and I was told that the sales team were in a meeting.

I waited a reasonable time, and since I had not received a callback from the salesperson I wanted, I called the company again. I was told the same thing; the sales team was in a meeting. This time, I asked the lady at reception to send an urgent message to my usual salesperson. It was Friday afternoon, and time was running out to place the order.

I heard nothing for almost an hour, so I escalated matters. Rather than go to a competitor, I chose to call the C.E.O. of the company I preferred to deal with. I explained that I did not wish to get anyone into trouble, but the situation demanded immediate action because my repeated attempts to buy products from them were being ignored. I told him everything that had happened, and within 4 minutes of ending our phone call, my usual sales guy called me. I placed my order, and he made his entire monthly sales target in a single 20-minute phone call.

He also told me that he had been given the urgent message and all the other notes about me calling and needing urgent attention regarding a sale. Amazingly, the new sales manager thought it better for the sales team to complete his latest training course rather than actually sell something to a customer.

It would have been obvious even to a 10-year-old child that selling something to someone always comes before sitting around and talking about how to generate more sales. Anyone who has ever run their own business knows that the customer is king and always will be.

I often wonder how many similar meetings take place each day in companies all over the world while the company is struggling to increase sales. I am sure that everyone who reads these words can remember attending at least one worthless meeting at some point.

Typically, the most useless meeting is a committee meeting. It could be a homeowners committee, a corporate committee, or even worse, a local government committee. No matter who convenes it, most committee meetings are completely bogged down by personality, ineffectual protocol, and poor leadership.

A local government authority in England convened a perfect example of a completely ludicrous meeting. Fortunately, the British tabloid press made the meeting infamous, so it became highly embarrassing for the local authority concerned. My special prize for holding the most useless committee meeting to date is awarded to Gloucester County Council in the U.K.

Unbelievably, this idiotic council once convened a planning committee meeting to decide if they should include a simple paper napkin when delivering meals to house-bound senior citizens! The result of this pointless, stupid, and insulting meeting was that a complete risk-assessment study had to be made at the taxpayer's expense regarding using and, more importantly, the potential dangers posed by paper napkins! This is sad but true. It is also an excellent real-world example of what a completely useless meeting can be about.

If the council leadership had been strong and possessed even a modicum of common sense, then the whole thing would have been dismissed in the early stages as being completely unnecessary. Basic common sense and good leadership skills seemed utterly absent in Gloucester Town Hall. Perhaps these elements were not in anyone's job description...

My own rule of committees and committee meetings states that the greater the number of members who sit on a committee, the greater its ability to be effective. In other words, the more people sitting on a committee, the less chance it has of reaching a quick and/or sensible decision.

Tips to Help Maximise Meetings

How do you ensure you get the most out of every meeting and achieve your desired objectives? How do you end your meeting with the attendees feeling that they have complete clarity of thought regarding your message and objective? Here is my checklist to help you maximise your meetings.

- Only convene a meeting when necessary.
- Never convene a meeting simply for the sake of it, perhaps as some form of reassurance.
- If the meeting ceases to be needed, cancel it immediately so that everyone's time is not wasted.
- Be sure to have a clearly defined objective for the outcome of the meeting. Stick to your agenda and set a time limit for each item.
- If possible, schedule your meeting with enough time in advance to allow all attendees to be completely prepared.
- Invite only those people who need to attend the meeting; do not waste the time of people who are not essential.
- Lead the meeting yourself or appoint a strong leader who will drive it through. If you do not, then your meeting might end up as a disorganised group discussion.
- You always have the option of adding a Q & A session at the end if you think it appropriate.
- Tell everyone to switch off their phones so they are not distracted by social media, personal messages, etc. It is rude for anyone in a meeting to always glance at and check their mobile phone unless it is integral to the meeting.
- Always start your meeting on time. If you do, it will usually end on time. Latecomers can play catch-up.
- Set a projected time limit for the meeting, and then divide that by two. Longer meetings usually fail to hold the attention span of the attendees, and they never usually achieve much more than what can be achieved in a shorter meeting.
- Be sure to end your meeting on time and avoid the urge to let it run over schedule. All attendees will very much appreciate this.

Time in Your Toolbox

Time, timing, and timekeeping are not just mere concepts but powerful tools when used strategically. In this case study, I will delve into the unconventional use of time as a strategic tool in crisis resolution. I will share a true story of how we engaged a formidable opponent for a client, using time, timing, and timekeeping as our most essential weapons.

Some years ago, a friend asked me to help his company with a serious problem. It was a medium-sized business in London, England, with a workforce of around 100 people. The company's order book was extremely healthy, but it had a significant cash flow problem.

This had been caused by suffering a series of bad debts due to rogue clients going out of business, which left them with a string of unpaid invoices in their wake. Unsurprisingly, the main problem was the enormous pressure created by the poor, almost non-existent cash flow. The person running the business was a man of honour, and he was keen to ensure that all his creditors were paid promptly.

The problems were further intensified because their major creditor had lost confidence. They were gambling that it would be better to call in the debt by instructing receivers to liquidate the company. More importantly, this was in the full knowledge that doing so would seriously affect the lives of the 100 employees who would probably lose their jobs as a result. This was a real crisis, and I could not let the lives of all those families be affected negatively, especially for the sake of waiting only a few more days to finally get paid.

As usual, in such circumstances, the company's bankers were as much use as a parachute would be on a submarine, so they did not offer any help. I was now faced with a hostile creditor, no cash flow, the jobs of 100 people at risk, and I had virtually no weapons to use except for time. A close assessment of the balance sheet and information clearly showed that the company would soon be solvent again and out of danger. All I had to do was hold off the angry creditor until outstanding invoices were finally paid, which would resolve the matter.

In those days, certain laws allowed companies to appoint an administrator to handle their affairs in such circumstances. I knew that going into administration would delay liquidators being called in by the creditor. I also knew that voluntary administration meant that we could select an administrator. Theoretically, this could provide the opportunity I needed to solve the problem. However, I needed to make sure the time of the meeting and the timing of events worked to our advantage.

I eventually found a friendly administrator willing to work toward the greater good. Someone who wanted to solve the problem rather than create a more significant problem by letting the company fold and making the workforce redundant.

Naturally, I wanted to choose the ground to engage my opponents. Since I had appointed the administrator, I could decide the time and place of the big meeting. Time and timing were vital, so I ensured that the meeting would take place on a Friday afternoon and at the latest time allowable on the day. I also chose a location near the south-central London office where we were working.

I also knew that the company I was helping had several other office locations dotted around the country. However, one of these locations, in particular, caught my attention when I was devising my plan. This was a tiny office servicing the Scottish region in a town called Berwick-upon-Tweed, which is officially the northernmost town in England.

In the lead-up to the meeting, my next tactical move was to carefully time the delivery of messages and information to all parties concerned. I had arranged for a message to be sent from the Scottish division of the company, which explained that some extremely urgent matters had to be dealt with right away.

I also knew the rules about timing in this respect, so I ensured that all communications were delivered within the legally accepted time so that we could still maintain control of where and when the meeting would take place. I knew that the administrator would have to call for a last-minute change of location because of the message from the Scottish division.

This changed everything. Instead of the administration meeting in the easy-to-reach location in South Central London, it was now to take place in Berwick-upon-Tweed, one of the most challenging places to get to at short notice. I had already checked into various forms of public transport and road journey times to ensure that it was almost impossible for anyone to attend the meeting at such short notice. The angry creditor could do absolutely nothing about this change of plan, and they had to accept the official location change in good faith.

Everything had turned out exactly as I had planned, which was good news for everyone concerned. The sizeable outstanding invoice had already been paid by the time a new meeting was agreed upon in a more convenient location. This meant that the angry creditor was paid in full, and confidence was restored. Furthermore, the workforce remained blissfully unaware that their jobs were ever in serious jeopardy. This was all achieved through the effective use of time, timing, and timekeeping as part of my Mental Martial Arts toolbox.

Timekeeping and Excuses

Does good timekeeping matter? Absolutely. Continual bad timekeeping is just bad manners. Being continually late sends the signal to those you are meeting that they are not important to you. You should always be on time if you want to be professional, care about others, and display good manners.

Naturally, everyone occasionally falls foul of circumstances beyond their control; this is just part of life. Modern road traffic can be completely unpredictable, and trains and planes might be delayed due to unforeseen weather or mechanical issues. Most people will have no problems accepting you being late occasionally due to such circumstances. If you find that you will be unavoidably late, you should always give people as much notice as possible.

If you call as soon as you are aware of a problem arising, your communication will always be greatly appreciated. However, nothing you can say will be appreciated or believed if you demonstrate consistently poor timekeeping. You will lose both credibility and respect, which are hard to win back.

What can you do to begin correcting your poor timekeeping habits? What can you do if you seem to live in your own time zone, away from the rest of the world? Here are a few ideas about how to change things for the better.

- Stop your negative self-talk, which reinforces your poor timekeeping. By continually affirming your bad timekeeping qualities, you are simply reinforcing your negative actions and conditioning your mind to accept them as normal. Use the caveat technique to correct this and help reprogram your mind to become an excellent timekeeper.
- Set your watch and other clocks a little ahead of the actual time, but only a few minutes ahead. Anything more than a few minutes, and you will always remember that the clock is set fast, so it will not help. If it is only a few minutes fast, you will soon forget about it. The result will be that you will usually find yourself with valuable time to spare.
- Make a conscious effort to be more aware of your time, what you need to do next and when.
- Leave post-it notes in unusual places to help remind you of your schedule. The notes can say something as simple as checking the time. Whatever they are, they do not need to be complicated.
- Set yourself a time limit to complete certain tasks, and then deliberately reduce the time that you initially set. Decreasing the

deadline will tend to make you more efficient, which usually generates some time to spare.
- Get to bed earlier in the evening. This simple action always helps to start each new day well. You will usually wake more refreshed, perhaps even ahead of time.
- Plan in detail and remember the axiom of the multiple Ps: Planning and Preparation Prevent Poor Performance. They also help prevent poor timekeeping.
- If you are travelling with others who need to leave home early in the morning to meet at the airport, use a simple call-back system. A call-and-call-back system is where each person who is travelling calls the others in an agreed sequence. Everyone who has received a call then calls the original caller back to show that they are awake. Just allow the phone to ring a couple of times; this way, no one even needs to answer a call. Calls are supported by a text message reminding the group who is calling whom next, and who has or has not responded, etc. If one person continually fails to answer, then call their home number or their spouse's cell phone, or leave even earlier to physically call at their home and bang on their door.

Good timekeeping is not that difficult to achieve and maintain. It also has the added benefit of helping to reduce both personal and business stress. It will help you get more done each day and demonstrate to others that they are important to you and that you respect them. More importantly, you will never again appear arrogant or rude simply because of your poor timekeeping.

Quote:

"The journey through life is like the sands of time in an hourglass; the nearer you get to the end, the quicker the sand seems to disappear."

Chapter 11 Summary – Power Moves:

武 *Toolbox Tactics are powerful weapons for the Mental Martial Artist.*

武 *Your toolbox can be used in limitless combinations; the choice of how to use it is always yours.*

Chapter 11 Summary – Pressure Points:

武 *Only convene essential meetings.*

武 *Time, timing, and timekeeping can be immensely powerful weapons.*

Chapter 12:
Success - A Journey, NOT A Destination

To succeed in life, love, and business, you must go far beyond what is ordinary. Ordinary is comfortable, and there is always a certain degree of solace found in the company of those who live by choice in their ordinary world.

I have never been satisfied with anything ordinary. I have always preferred the extraordinary in everything, which is almost certainly why I could achieve my World Records.

You can do the same or more if you genuinely want to. Find the courage within you to make your dreams a reality. Just believe in yourself and your abilities.

Never forget that your dreams never die on their own; each of us must deliberately kill them for them to die.

When choosing the extraordinary instead of the ordinary, you will occasionally encounter the hollow cachinnations of the less evolved. Their negativity usually has nothing to do with you or what you are doing; it typically reflects how they feel about themselves and their limitations.

If you believe, then you can achieve. It is that simple. Stretching yourself beyond the ordinary will always be a little daunting, but it is worth it in the end.

Many people fear change, but change is almost always your friend, so always embrace it. The rules that set specific accepted parameters in life, love, and business must sometimes be stretched or even broken to set new standards of excellence and achievement.

Past successes and achievements are simply that, the past. Your current successes and achievements are merely a new layer in your life's journey. Each layer should be a new starting point for even more significant successes and achievements.

If you do not continually build on your successes and achievements, then whatever you have achieved will soon become history.

Furthermore, you may even inadvertently slip into mediocrity. In the proverbial blink of an eye, you can easily find yourself following the standards set by others instead of being the one who sets the standards for everyone else to follow.

"Now, this is not the end. It is not even the beginning of the end. But it is, perhaps, the end of the beginning."

Sir Winston Churchill - November 1942.

www.BrianSterlingVete.com – www.HelenRenee.com

Other books by Brian Sterling-Vete and Helen Renée Wuorio

Usui Reiki Level One

An introduction to Reiki, covering its history and supporting science, is presented in an easy step-by-step format. This book and others in the series are course manuals for our online or in-person students.

Usui Reiki Level Two

The Reiki Level Two course advances your journey, teaching Power Symbols and their usage. It excludes the history and science from book one and is structured logically in a clear, step-by-step format, guiding you on what to do next.

Usui Reiki Level Three

The Level Three Master Teacher course finalises the journey for Level Two practitioners. It focuses solely on Level Three concepts, excluding the history and science from Book One, and is organised in a step-by-step format.

Usui Reiki Compendium – Levels One and Two

The Reiki Compendium is a complete book of our Usui Reiki Level One and Two courses, ideal for anyone wanting to progress through all levels of their Reiki Journey. It also serves as a manual for our online or in-person students.

Usui Reiki for Treating Animals

The Usui Reiki for Animals book is perfect for practitioners of all levels wanting to learn safe and effective animal treatment techniques. It also highlights differences in animal chakras and energy centres unique to specific animals.

Usui Reiki Protection

This is the complete guide to spiritual protection, negative energy clearing, smudging, and exorcism. It is an essential resource for every paranormal investigator and anyone wishing to clear people and places of negative energy.

Muscle-up For Menopause

Menopause is inevitable, so take control. Brief, intense exercises with minimal recovery demands and a high-protein plant-based diet significantly impact your experience during menopause.

Paranormal Investigation - The Black Book of Scientific Ghost Hunting

It contains a special scientific critical path graphic page to work from and a step-by-step guide to a complete paranormal investigation. It also advises you on how to protect yourself from malevolent paranormal entities.

The 70 Second Difference - Politically Incorrect, Occasionally Amusing, and Brutally Effective

A science-based guide to the most efficient ways to exercise and build muscle and strength. Just 70 seconds of focused exercise daily can provide a total-body workout.

The ISOmetric Bible - Exercise Anywhere with Scientifically Proven Isometrics

A complete, scientific, and user-friendly benchmark book about scientifically proven isometric exercises: no special equipment is needed for a total-body workout.

TRISOmetrics - Advanced Science-Based High-Intensity Strength and Muscle Building

This advanced, high-intensity exercise system combines three proven techniques into a powerful new approach, with or without equipment, while travelling or in the gym.

The TRISO90 Course – Advanced Strength and Muscle Building with The TRISOmetrics System
A 90-day step-by-step advanced bodybuilding and strength-training course combining three science-based principles performed with or without equipment or in a gym routine.

Workout at Work - Exercise at Work Without Anyone Even Knowing What You're Doing! Time is the #1 reason why people don't exercise. The average person spends over ten years of their working life at a desk! Isometric exercises let you work out effectively without leaving your desk.

The ISO90 Course – The 12-Week/90-Day Shape-up and Get Strong Course. A complete step-by-step 90-day/12-week isometric body shaping, bodybuilding, and strength-building course is ideal for both beginners and advanced.

Isometric Power Exercises for Martial Arts - Build Superior Strength, Muscle and Martial Arts 'Firepower' Using the Proven System Bruce Lee Used. This book is a valuable resource for practical isometric exercises that build serious strength, muscle, and martial arts firepower.

Improvised Isometric Exercise Devices - The Daisy Chain
Improvised Isometric Exercise Devices, or IIEDs, come in all shapes and sizes, limited only by your imagination. This is a resource for practical exercises that can be performed and for learning how to extend the daisy chain safely.

Improvised Isometric Exercise Devices - The Climber's Sling
IIEDs come in all shapes and sizes and are only limited by your imagination. This valuable resource lists practical isometric exercises that can be performed and how to safely extend the climber's sling.

The Bullworker Bible - The Ultimate Science-Based Guide to The Classic Personal Multi-Gym. Approved by The Bullworker makers (and Steel Bow®), it is the companion to The Bullworker 90™ Course. It is a complete, science-based, and user-friendly book for maximum results.

The Bullworker 90™ Course - The Ultimate Science-Based 12-Week/90-Day Get Strong and Grow Muscle Course Approved by The Bullworker makers, this complete 90-day course and companion book to The Bullworker Bible,

The Bullworker Compendium - The Bullworker Bible and The Bullworker90 Course Combined Approved by the makers of The Bullworker. The Bullworker Compendium™ combines both The Bullworker Bible™ and The Bullworker 90™ Course in a single huge book.

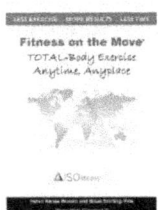
Fitness on the Move - Enjoy Gym-Quality Workout Sessions ANYWHERE! This book lists practical exercises that can be performed while travelling almost anywhere and in any vehicle. If there is enough space to sit down and/or stand upright, you can perform a total-body workout!

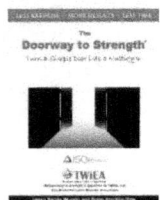
The Doorway to Strength - Turn a Door into a Strength-Building Multigym. It shows how a simple door, doorway, and frame can create a multi-gym of exercises using the amazing Iso-Bow®. Required: 2 x Iso-Bows®, a solid door and frame, and a door wedge/stop.

Feel Better In 70 Seconds
Studies show that brief exercise combats depression without significant cost or time. Just 70 seconds of continuous movement allows a full-body workout using isometric exercises, requiring 2 x Iso-Bows®.

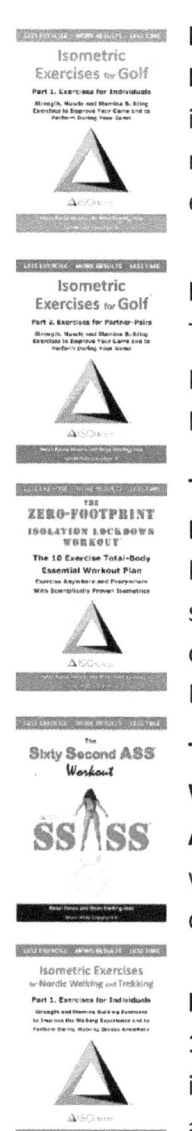

Isometric Exercises for Golf Part 1. Exercises for Individuals. Isometric exercises can turn a round of golf into a full-body workout at each hole, using a golf club as a makeshift exercise tool. Part 1 provides customised exercises to improve swing power for individual needs.

Isometric Exercises for Golf Part 2. Partner-Pairs
The companion to Book 1 focuses on exercises best performed in partnered pairs during breaks, games, or practice sessions.

The Zero-Footprint Isolation Lockdown Workout - The 10 Exercise Total-Body Essential Workout. Ten essential total-body exercises can be done anywhere; if you can stand or sit, you can have a powerful workout in just 70 seconds a day! NOTE: This is a variation of The 70 Second Difference™.

The Sixty Second ASS Workout - The Ultimate 60-Second Workout to Shape, Tone, Lift, and Get the Backside You've Always Wanted. The fastest and most effective "ass" workout ever devised. Scientifically proven exercises deliver a no-nonsense, time-efficient workout.

Isometric Exercises for Nordic Walking and Trekking - Part 1. Exercises for Individuals. Perform gym-quality total-body isometric exercises during walk breaks with walking poles as an Improvised Isometric Exercise Device. Book 1 serves as an exercise resource guide for individuals.

Isometric Exercises for Nordic Walking and Trekking - Part 2. Exercises for Walk Partner-Pairs
This is the companion to Book 1 and focuses on exercises best performed as a partner pair with a friend.

Being American Married to a Brit - An Amusing Guide for Anglo-American Couples. This quirky, fun-filled roller coaster ride is about how even the most basic everyday transatlantic conversations can bring laughter. It's dedicated to all transatlantic couples.

Mental Martial Arts - Intellectual Life and Business Combat Skills. An intellectual language and combat skills system based on martial arts principles. Learn to guide and redirect the energy of influential individuals and large organisations to achieve goals.

Tuxedo Warriors
The companion book to The Tuxedo Warrior expands on the story, serving as both a biography and autobiography of cult author Cliff Twemlow. It also includes unique insights from Brian Sterling-Vete.

The Tuxedo Warrior by Cliff Twemlow – Prologue and epilogue by Brian Sterling-Vete. A doorman navigates respect with diplomacy or force, managing nightlife's challenges. It's a balancing act, depicting peaceful resolutions or violent clashes and providing a raw glimpse into a vibrant yet perilous world of clubland peacekeeping.

The Pike by Cliff Twemlow – Prologue and epilogue by Brian Sterling-Vete. A monstrous pike terrorises Lake Windermere, attacking people and boats and causing panic. Some traders exploit the chaos, hindering the creature's capture to profit as the terror escalates.

The Beast of Kane by Cliff Twemlow – Prologue and epilogue by Brian Sterling-Vete. The Gordon family invites darkness by adopting a stray Elkhound, igniting ancient evil prophecies. Kane faces supernatural terror, from animal attacks to gruesome murder, as a chilling winter amplifies the fear in town.

The Haunting of Lilford Hall - The Birthplace of the United States as a Nation Haunted by the Man Behind The Pilgrim Fathers. A baffling case of paranormal activity occurred from 2012 to 2013, involving multiple people. Robert Browne, who got the Pilgrim Fathers to sail on The Mayflower in 1620, is believed to haunt Lilford Hall.

Paranormal Dictionary

This comprehensive guide covers the most common paranormal terminology, entities, and equipment used during investigations, along with a few enduring mysteries for good measure. It is ideal for both new and experienced investigators.

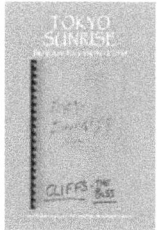

Tokyo Sunrise Background Story and Movie Script

Tokyo Sunrise is one of Cliff Twemlow's famous film concepts. The renowned cinematographer Robert Foster filmed extensively to produce a promotional video sizzle reel, aiming to sell the movie to potential investors. This also tells the story of the Richard Gere connection.

Hair Transplantation and Restoration

Hair Transplantation and Restoration is the essential guide to hair loss, growth, and ALL forms of hair transplantation and restoration. It is a collaboration between Brian Sterling-Vete and Malcolm Mendelsohn, the world's #1 independent expert with almost 50 years of experience.

Tarot – The Complete Guide

Explore the ultimate tarot guide, covering its history, card styles, and meanings. Master the art and science of tarot reading with insights and secret techniques from an internationally acclaimed Tarot Master, Helen Renée.

Tarot Card Spreads
Discover the ultimate tarot spread guide, featuring various spreads for love, money, career, business, and key life decisions. It includes detailed diagrams and descriptions to enhance your tarot practice.

Quantum Paranormal
Quantum physics meets the paranormal, offering fascinating explanations about the existence of paranormal phenomena and the mechanisms underpinning them. This deeply controversial book also challenges a crucial belief at the foundation of the Christian Church.

www.BrianSterlingVete.com – www.HelenRenee.com